Advance Praise for *Simple Serenity*

"In the seemingly ceaseless cacophony of life today this book reminds us that the necessary grounding of mind, body and spirit is possible when we take the time to contemplate what really matters: the nurturing energy of insight that flows from within.

Sometimes it takes a sage guide to lead us through the distractions of our daily lives: Nancy's book of meditative insights takes us where we need to go to stay the course of life on life's terms."

—William Moyers, VP Public Affairs and Community Relations, Hazelden Betty Ford Foundation, author of *Broken, Now What?*, and *A New Day, A New Life.*

"What Nancy Oelklaus has given us in this book is not only razor sharp check-ins for our personal life but also powerful insights for how to start our day over when we are out of sorts. If I can be so bold, this lady disappears within these pages so that Universal Truths might shine through with purity and simplicity. This treasure will make a good platform for a book study group."

—Albert Clayton Gaulden, author of *Signs and Wonders* and *You're Not Who You Think You Are*

"I edited this book for the publisher while running an online positive psychology course. In that course, I use two of my own books as references: students are required to read a specific section from one or another before a session, and another after. While working through *Simple Serenity*, I have realized that I could use it equally well as the textbook. Everything within it is the wisdom of the ages, and everything within it has been demonstrated as effective through research on positive psychology."

—Bob Rich, author, *From Depression to Contentment*

"Peace. Serenity. Throughout the ages, great spiritual teachers have offered us these pathways to survival in a world troubled, grieving, and afraid. In this same tradition, Nancy Oelklaus shares her personal journey to quiet places in the heart. In language both beautiful and simple, she gently guides the reader into shifts in perspective, out of storms and into safe havens. Out of exhaustion and anxiety into balance and gratitude. Out of unrest into loving mindfulness. *Simple Serenity*, a soft light of hope and inspiration, is to be read and re-read. Oelklaus is more than a teacher. She is a wise friend and a comfort. A treasure."

—Helen Delaney, author of *The Messenger: The Improbable Story of a Grieving Mother and a Spirit Guide*

"Dr. Nancy, as I've always known her—first my client, later hers, and ultimately, trusted colleagues. Great friends from the beginning. It hit hard when I learned of her plans to leave Texas. Initially, a sense of loss, until she began blogging her *Journey from Head to Heart*. I read every one. Shared widely to fellow seekers. Often responded to her gracious invitation to express myself—and *always* received a thoughtful reply. Now, the *Simple Serenity* meditation collection! Will savor her inspirational wisdom going forward—from head to heart."

—Lucky Lindy Segall, Fredericksburg, Texas

"I have been on my intentional spiritual trek for almost 40 years of the 78 years that I have been blessed to live. I have chosen this life because the world has been such a challenging place to live as an African American woman. My heart and soul knew that there had to be another way, while still honoring my gratitude for being a Black woman in America.

Living in fear of injustice and prejudice was the way of the world for people of color. It has been very challenging to grow to love who I am with confidence, grace, humility, and gratitude. I found this fear-based reality in everything and everywhere I lived and traveled in the USA. But, in the serene nature of Sedona's Red Rock Country, I was able to refocus and gain a stronger sense of myself as a Black woman and as a spiritual person. And, after over 20 years of being in Sedona, I realized that I had learned many of the lessons that Nancy puts before us in *Simple Serenity*, and I could leave and take these lessons of the Red Rocks with me.

"I realized that the dichotomy of life shows us both sides of the coin – always – if we can stop, be still, and reflect on what is actually before us. I have come to understand and know that EVERY single experience is a lesson. I believe that is the big lesson that Nancy is calling us to consider – both sides of the big questions that LIFE puts before us. Which will we choose? I believe that she is calling us to live our life for the HIGHEST GOOD. Sit in the stillness and consider SIMPLE SERENITY for your life every single day."

Sarah Payne Naylor, author of *Crossing Rough Waters: A Journey from Fear to Freedom* and *COVID-19 TOOLKIT: Mindfully Manage Stress and Anxiety*.

Simple Serenity
Finding Joy in Your Life

Nancy Oelklaus, Ed. D.

Loving Healing Press

Ann Arbor, MI

Learn more at www.NancyOelklaus.com

ISBN 978-1-61599-663-6 paperback
ISBN 978-1-61599-664-3 hardcover
ISBN 978-1-61599-665-0 eBook

Loving Healing Press
5145 Pontiac Trail
Ann Arbor, MI 48105

www.LHPress.com   Tollfree 888-761-6268
info@LHPress.com   FAX 734-663-6861

Distributed by Ingram (USA/CAN/AU), Bertram's Books
(UK/EU), New Leaf Distributing (USA).

Audiobook edition available from Audible.com and iTunes

Dedication

In Thornton Wilder's play, *Our Town*, the character Emily, from her afterlife, says, "Oh, Earth, you're too wonderful for anybody to realize you. Do any human beings ever realize life while they live it—every, every minute?"

This morning as I journal, a gentle snow is falling. Looking out at the white beauty, my whole being fills with amazed gratitude. In this moment, I am realizing life while I live it.

This book is for those who want to join me and for my sister Carolyn in her afterlife.

Contents

Foreword iii

Welcoming Serenity 1

Getting to Healing 3

Chapter 1 - Moving from Here to There 5

Chapter 2 - Live in Gratitude 17

Chapter 3 - Understanding: Gateway to Acceptance 23

Chapter 4 - Be Joyful 43

Chapter 5 - Truth Simply Stands 55

Chapter 6 - Reconciliation 71

Chapter 7 - Love is Quiet 85

Chapter 8 - Be Still 101

Chapter 9 - Light Has Come into the World 117

Chapter 10 - Silent Striated Sentinel 125

Appendix 139

Author's Note 141

About the Author 143

About the Cover 145

About the Artist 147

Bibliography 149

Index 151

Foreword

Once in a lifetime, if you are very lucky, you may meet a special person who seems to have been put in your path to magnify the moments that make you feel alive. These individuals elevate the ordinary and sanctify the mundane with the lightest touch, and a bemusing smile. Somehow, you are gently invited to open up your heart to recollections of your own that have been long forgotten, shut away from the light in the recesses of dismissal, minimization, and forgetfulness. Such a person is the author of Simple Serenity, my dear friend, Nancy Oelklaus.

In this beautiful book, Nancy shows generosity of spirit as she shares with us perspectives she has allowed to develop within herself over years of living courageously, sweetly, and boldly. From the Dedication onward, Nancy extends to us a personal invitation not only to retrace the magical moments of discovery along her life journey, but also to reconsider our own unique pathways and their lessons for us. For Nancy, prose becomes poetry, and the reader is entrusted with reading between the lines.

Jan Ford Mustin, Ph.D., Psychologist
Peak Performance Institute,
A Professional Corporation

Welcoming Serenity

I was third in line at the grocery checkout. The woman in the middle was complaining, to no one in particular, about Sedona. "I hate this place," she said. "I can't wait to get out of here, and I'm moving tomorrow."

The woman first in line turned around with a bit of a smile. "In Sedona, we say that the energy we bring into this place gets amplified."

But many people coming to Sedona expect a miracle and are disappointed that one doesn't materialize.

My husband Harlan and I moved to Sedona, Arizona, in June of 2005, after a month-long vacation the January before. We simply fell in love with the Village of Oak Creek, and before we left to go back home to Austin, Texas, we had bought a house.

In 1991 I began a personal journey that I wrote about in *Journey from Head to Heart: Living and Working Authentically*, sharing the specific tools and processes I used, as well as my transformative experiences. I had worked diligently to shift out of negative, self-defeating thinking into a way of being that fused religion, spirituality and science. I was a truly happy person, with a very strong support system. The only question I had about the move we were anticipating was the loss of that support system.

Of course, I didn't lose it. Those people and ways of being did not leave me. They moved with me, and I began to open even wider to the majesty of the red rocks, the blue sky and the white clouds—to appreciate the desert and all of its creatures.

Today, Harlan and I often hike Red Rock Pathway, near Bell Rock, which is said to be one of the strongest vortexes in Sedona. One day we came upon a woman stopped on the trail, leaning against the rocks, with the palms of her hands lifted to the sky. As we neared, we could hear her wail, "I can't feel it," expecting us to tell her how to find the vortex energy.

The secret of Sedona is that you bring your energy into it, and the vortexes all around amplify it.

The Sedona vortex expert I most trust is Pete Sanders. His weekly presentations share keys that help seekers maximize their meditations and experiences of the energy of the vortexes. His book, *Scientific Vortex Information,* enlightens about how to engage with vortex energy.

Sanders writes, "To maximize your experience in the vortexes you need to have an attitude of allowing, while you explore, focus and guide your awareness, rather than forcing...You have to allow it to come to you" (p. 34)

In this spirit, I offer the meditations in this book. May you allow their energy to come to you.

In making this offering, I don't mean to imply that I never have a bad day or a negative thought. I have simply learned that, no matter where I am, I have a choice. Each of my reflections is followed by an opportunity for the reader to write or draw a response. In a sense, you are a co-author of this book. You'll get out of it what you put into it.

This book is to be savored, not devoured. What's written here won't change your life—unless you participate, absorb and respond to the words from your heart. Then, get ready to live the life you truly want.

Getting to Healing

On Valentine's Day 2022 I saw a piece in the *Washington Post* by Brittany Long Olsen. She posed the question "How do you wish you had been loved as a kid?" She suggested that couples answer this question together and agree to give what was missing in the past to their partner today.

I thought this was a great question, so I posed it to my daughter. She thought for a long while and then said, "I worked through all of that, and I no longer feel that something was missing."

In other words, she had been through the process of awareness, acceptance, and forgiveness, and she is free from resentment for the mistakes and oversights of her father and me while she was growing up.

Don't just read this book. Process it by writing, drawing, painting, making a collage or vision board, sculpting, working with clay. As you, in your own way, work through the prompts for processing the passages, may you experience whatever healing or forgiveness is there for you.

Chapter 1 - Moving from Here to There

When we traveled, my husband Harlan and I would often play "let's pretend" while he was playing golf and I was driving the cart. One of us would ask, "I wonder what it would be like to live here?" Then we would imagine ourselves living in that place as he finished eighteen holes. At the end of his play, one of us would say, "Nah. I think we'll just stay where we are."

Where we were at that time is Austin, Texas, a fast-growing, technology-rich center. We loved Austin for so many reasons, chief of which was our home on the rim of a canyon on the eastern edge of the Texas Hill Country.

Our favorite vacation spot was Sedona. After we had visited there for about five years, we decided to stay for a whole month in a condo in the Village of Oak Creek, which is about five miles south of Sedona. One day as we were driving along, he started our game—except this time his words were different. He said, "I think I could live here."

I replied, "I've been thinking the same thing."

The next day we were on the golf course. I was the driver. When we got to the fifth fairway, I looked to my right and saw a "for sale" sign. I drove over to pick up one of the flyers. Long story short, today we live in that house. Our decision wasn't a straight path. There was another house that Harlan thought was "a deal," so he gave a low offer, which was rejected when another offer for the asking price was made. But that's another story.

The main point is that we decided to move from Austin, Texas to the Village of Oak Creek, AZ. From a population of around a million to around 6,000. Big change.

Yet, not a change at all. While I lived in Austin, I made a decision to live from my heart, to focus on myself and not the behavior of others, and to live with intention. Conscious living, you might call it.

Conscious living is a state of being, not a place. But because geographical move is a major stressor for most people, I'll start with that transition.

1-1: From Chaos to Peace

Our decision to sell our house in Austin and move to Sedona has thrown my surroundings into a jumble, as, daily, workers swarm in to prepare the house to sell. Furniture that belongs in this room has been moved to that room for staging purposes. Boxes of framed family photos and other familiar items from shelves are packed and stored. I won't see them again for months. Furnishings are clustered in the center of rooms.

Turmoil is the best way to describe what's going on with me, and I'm laughing at myself as I realize the one who teaches others to find their calm center and live from there is having difficulty practicing what she teaches. Instead, the reverse has happened. My inner peace has been disturbed by my jumbled surroundings.

To make it through, in addition to morning meditation, I've increased my conscious awareness. Do I need a drink of water? How about a walk? A short nap? Reading just for enjoyment?

As I pull into myself and meet my own needs, the external disarray becomes less significant, and I begin to find peace again.

Last night I simply shampooed my hair and as I awoke this morning, I felt simple pleasure in the awareness of clean hair.

Exercise 1-1: When chaos surrounds you, what do you do?

1-2: Equanimity at the Car Wash

I strive for equanimity, the ability to stay even-keeled, regardless of what's happening. To be kind, even when others around you are exploding. To be calm and clear-headed, even in the face of danger. To be true to myself when it might be tempting to conform.

I've made some progress towards equanimity, but yesterday I lost it. When Harlan and I returned home from a month away, a remodeling project that should have been finished had taken over our home. Realizing I couldn't sleep in my own bed and had nowhere to hang my clothes, I lost equanimity. First, I exploded at my innocent husband and then at the unsuspecting contractor.

The next day I drove my construction-dust-covered car through a quick car wash. I guided the car to the conveyor track and, as instructed, put it in neutral, took my hands off the wheel, and my foot off the brake.

Then I put my head back and closed my eyes. I heard the water pelting the car, but I was dry. I heard the softer sound of soap. Then the brushes went to work. Water again. Finally, a long blast of drying air as my car completed its gentle movement through the process.

The cleaning had happened around me as I simply sat at rest, protected, eyes closed.

I realized I lose equanimity when I am displeased. But when I enclose myself within a safe space, put my gear in neutral, take my hands off the wheel and my foot off the brake, peace rules.

Exercise 1-2: What steals you from equanimity? What keeps you in it?

1-3: Leaving

As I look out toward the canyon in the gray morning mist, I know it's time to leave.

The oak tree that was just a sapling when we moved here has grown so tall that slowly and inexorably, it has taken the center of the canyon view. In winter, when the leaves are gone, the view emerges through the bare branches. Now that it's spring again, green leaves prevail.

I chose this house for that view. I liked its other qualities, as well, but it was the view I most loved.

Over the years, we terraced and planted the part of the canyon slope that is ours. With the plantings, we pulled nature closer until now, we are immersed in its exquisite beauty.

It feels complete and whole. Gently and lovingly, I give thanks and release.

Exercise 1-3: What in your life feels complete and whole? For what are you giving thanks and releasing?

1-4: Done Too Soon

What are the words that describe my feelings as I prepare to leave Austin, where I've lived for 25 years? Here I started two new careers. Here Harlan and I met and married. Here I've loved living as I've worked with many people to find emotional and spiritual health.

One of those people emailed me last week, expressing her feelings about my leaving. Her words evoked sadness, and what immediately came to my mind were the lyrics from Neil Diamond, "And wept when it was all done, for being done too soon." I shed some tears, but it didn't feel right to grieve. There hadn't been a death.

Then I ran across these words from Rabindranath Tagore: "When old words die out on the tongue, new melodies break forth from the heart; and where the old tracks are lost, new country is revealed with its wonders."

Our move is more arrival than departure, and my true feeling is deep gratitude for the relationships and opportunities that Austin has so generously given, mixed with joyful anticipation of what the future holds in Sedona.

Exercise 1-4: Exercise: Right now, with whatever is going on, how do you feel?

1-5: Disappointment

By intention and design, I live a happy, peaceful life. Not having expectations and enjoying life one moment at a time is how I try to live.

But yesterday I was living the sentiment expressed in these lines from Emily Dickinson: "A great hope fell. You heard no noise. The ruin was within."

Harlan and I made an offer on a house that had been on the market for almost a year—a house with some issues due to its age, but redeemed by a fabulous, panoramic view. We went for it. Unfortunately, on the same day, someone else submitted a higher bid, and of course the owner accepted it. A great hope fell. I went silent. So did Harlan. Finally, I was able to say, "I'm sad."

Previously I would have brushed my feelings aside, said, "Oh, well," and pushed ahead, refusing to feel. But today I have come to understand that it's better for me to feel the feeling and move through it. Perhaps the truest statement I made was to our realtor. I said, "We're heartbroken. Give us some time and we'll try again."

Today is a new day, and I'm grateful for the experience Harlan and I had together as we went through the process of making the offer. I choose to believe there's another house for us that will meet all of our needs, one where we can live happily. And that's the most important thing.

P.S. We've been in the home we actually bought for about 7 years. The view is just as fabulous, and the house is much better suited for our lifestyle. The house we lost the bid on now has its view obstructed by tall trees planted by a new homeowner on the block.

Exercise 1-5: How do you handle disappointment?

1-6: Solution for Overwhelm

In the state of overwhelm is where I've been. We are moving from a house we've lived in for nineteen years, so we're weeding and packing while finishing a remodel and preparing the house for sale.

In the last two weeks we have worked with a realtor, contractor, paint consultant, and stager, each of which gave us a long list of tasks to do. I was relieved when I realized we had heard from everyone we needed to hear from.

The state of overwhelm is confusion and chaos. In it, I feel rudderless. I can't stay there for long.

So yesterday Harlan and I got a stack of index cards and wrote only one task to be completed on each card. We also wrote who is responsible for completing that task. Then we arranged the cards in the best sequence. Working together, we actually moved two cards to the "completed" stack.

Today I have a plan and a system for doing everything that needs to be done. The work has moved from contemplation to action. Our house will still be in chaos for the next two or three weeks, but I am at peace.

Exercise 1-6: What do you do when you're overwhelmed?

1-7: Lesson from a Ceiling Fan

When it comes to cleaning, I love telling other people what I want and then going for a pedicure while they do it.

With so much to do to get our house ready to sell, I've found myself with a dust cloth in my hand. I even sponge-mopped the deck with a cleaner that brings out the gold highlights in the wood. I love seeing that dry, dusty wood quench its thirst and glow.

But the ceiling fan on the deck—that's a different story. I pretend I don't see the dust, even though I know it's there. I asked the cleaning lady to clean it, which she happily agreed to do. Then she forgot. By the time I remembered to check it, she was gone.

For two days I did nothing. Then our realtor scheduled someone to see the house. All I could think about was that dirty ceiling fan.

Early in the morning on the day of the showing, I climbed onto the stepladder to reach the dreaded fan. To my surprise, the dirt lifted easily. In a very few minutes, I had a clean ceiling fan.

More importantly, I had faced a dread and completed a simple task. For the rest of the day, I had a sense of accomplishment. Then I went for a manicure.

Exercise 1-7: What are you dreading?

1-8: Just Gratitude

My grandmother gave birth to my dad, her eighth child, in a dugout with a dirt floor. Once I said to her, "Living like that must have been terribly difficult," as I tried to coax her story of a hardscrabble existence. She responded, "Oh, no. It wasn't hard at all. We had the most wonderful neighbors." Then she turned the story to acts of kindness she had experienced from those who lived nearby.

Grandmother always had an innate grateful, peaceful state of mind.

I, on the other hand, have to work at it. For many years my emotions were shut down, as I stressfully plowed my way through degrees and career advances. As I began to change, the first feelings that poured out were grief and anger.

Then I learned to express gratitude.

As I sit here in a half-empty house, making final preparation for our move to Sedona, I could slip into sadness or overwhelm. In fact, when that happened a few days ago, I called a friend to express my feelings. She asked, "What are you grateful for?" As I focused on what I'm grateful for, my gloom lifted until there was no darkness at all.

Exercise 1-8: What are you grateful for?

1-9: Lightly

All my framed awards have gone to recycle.
Walls are bare.
Even my old published articles went with them.
Shelves that held my past are empty.

Today I stand on the rim of tomorrow,

Seeing only glimpses of what the future holds.
Wherever the road leads, I'll walk it lightly.

Exercise 1-9: How lightly are you walking?

1-10: Rhythm

I knew the rhythm of my life in Austin so well. Easily, I floated in the familiar circles and cycles. When Harlan and I decided to move to Sedona, that rhythm changed. The mere decision shifted everything as the well-known patterns dissipated.

My calendar was blank. I had no cleaners or grocery store or hair stylist or dentist or doctor. I didn't know anyone. There was just me, flowing into the unexperienced.

Flowing has a rhythm all its own. Quiet silence. White space. My new rhythm.

Exercise 1-10: What is your rhythm today?

1-11: End of the Lists

For months I had lived from lists comprised of the tasks required for remodeling, selling, and buying a house. Then, of course, there were the tasks required for moving.

When I came to the end of the lists, my spirits sagged. I felt sad and useless.

My instinct when I'm feeling low is to stick my chin out and pretend that I'm okay. I tried that approach for a short time.

Then I remembered what I learned from a dear friend many years ago. Yield to my feelings. Name them. Feel them intensely, in a quiet place with no noise or distractions. Fully feel. Do what it takes to express the feelings. Then let them go.

Today I am refreshed as I sense possibility, make new friends, establish new routines, and create the life I want in this new place.

Exercise 1-11: What do you do when you come to the end of your lists?

1-12: Leaving Isn't Leaving

As I've thought about leaving the city that has been my home for 24 years, I've thought mostly about the friends I won't see as often. But I haven't felt sad, and I've wondered what's going on with me that I'm not sad.

I believe we exchange energy with people as we come and go. With friends, that is the energy of love and good will. Even when we are no longer in that person's presence, the energy we experienced with them lives on within us, ready to come to life again through memory. Thus, I'm not really leaving the friendships. Granted, I will have physical contact less frequently and less opportunity to make new memories. Even so, the love I have for these dear ones is not diminished.

One of the many gifts that Austin has given me is widening my circle of friends and teaching me how to be a better friend. For this, I am profoundly grateful.

Exercise 1-12: What is your experience with leaving?

1-13: Hostage Release

For almost two weeks our internet was out. During that time, Harlan or I were constantly on the phone with our provider, moving through their ineffective process. We said to each other, "This is the disadvantage of living in a small town. Sedona is not wired like Austin. This would never happen in Austin." We assumed we had to accept this terrible service.

My mood was disgruntled. It was the first of the month, and bills that I normally pay online were due. I needed to reconcile the bank account. All of my systems were on hold.

Then I realized I could take my iPad to the coffee shop and use their internet. But I resented it.

Then I realized I could choose to enjoy the coffee shop, with its music and activity, instead of being alone in my office at home.

Then I realized I could change internet providers. With one phone call, we had new, faster internet service installed within three hours. Finally, I was free.

Exercise 1-13: When have you felt as if you were being held hostage and your world was narrowing? How did you work your way out of it? How long did it take?

1-14: Wardrobe and Life

Once I worked with a style consultant to help me weed, replenish, and manage my wardrobe so that it supported the life I truly wanted to live. After our work together, I felt that my wardrobe contained the essentials for living in Austin, Texas.

Then I moved to Sedona, Arizona, and my lifestyle changed. I wasn't sure what I would need in this new life, so I left those Austin clothes in my closet for a year or so. Then I started weeding. I kept weeding. I weeded some more, without much replenishing.

When I decided to put away my winter clothes, a task that used to take a couple of hours in Austin was accomplished in about five minutes, as I moved things from one rack to another. Once again, I see the truth of what that consultant taught me—that my wardrobe is a reflection of my life. Today I am so grateful for the simplicity and peace all around me, reflected by my wardrobe.

A few days ago, I made a clothing purchase—three items. This morning I took four items to the thrift store. That's how simplicity works.

Exercise 1-14: What does your wardrobe say about your life? Is it what you want?

Chapter 2 - Live in Gratitude

Put your hand over your heart. Realize that this heart started beating in the third week after your conception. Ever since that moment, your heart has been faithfully pumping nourishment throughout your system, sustaining your life. So, through your hand, say "thank you" to your heart for so faithfully nourishing your life.

2-1: Gratitude

Quite a few years ago, when my life was in upheaval, I learned the simple practice of gratitude. Although I had two healthy, successful children, a good job, and many advantages, I did not know how to be truly grateful. I decided to practice. My first realization that I had made progress was one morning as I looked at the gas gauge in my car and felt, from my heart, true gratitude that I could afford gasoline.

Since that moment, I start every day with a gratitude list. It changes my perspective and gives me a good day, no matter what.

Today I am grateful for our democracy. I'm also grateful for a beautiful sunrise.

Exercise 2-1: What is your experience, from your heart, with gratitude?

2-2: Giving Thanks

As I load my dishwasher, I often think of my grand-mother, who didn't have running water, so she pumped water from a cistern to wash dishes. Yet she loaded the table for a large family with delicious foods—and always had cookies for me.

Then I think of my other grandmother. She invariably met us at the gate with, "I love you," which she repeated as we left. Her drumbeat was, "Get an education."

Then there's my mother, a kind woman whose pecan pie was legendary. I follow her recipe, which never fails.

For those who came before me, I am grateful. For those coming after me, I am grateful. For all the experiences of my life that brought me to today, I am grateful.

Exercise 2-2: For what are you grateful? Make your answer as complete as possible.

2-3; In the Moment

Early in the morning Harlan and I got up and drove into Sedona for a tax meeting with our accountant. It was a beautiful, sunny morning. We stopped for my favorite breakfast—Egg McMuffin at McDonald's. A few minutes early, we arrived at the accountant's office, prepared. All the blanks on the work sheet he had sent in advance were filled in. All the documentation for every category was neatly sorted. We left his office less than ten minutes after we arrived.

I remarked, "That was the easiest tax experience I've ever had." The day seemed even brighter. I simply savored the moment.

Exercise 2-3: So much of the time, we are thinking about what's next or waiting for "something big" instead of simply enjoying what is. When is the last time you had an "in the moment" experience?

2-4: Props and Daily Reminders

A quotation from *In Love with the World* by Jongey Ingyur Rinpoche jumped out at me: "Monastic robes help shelter the mind from straying into wrong views or incorrect behavior. They offer a constant reminder to stay here, stay aware."

Years ago, as I was making some life changes, someone gave me a James Avery gift certificate. With it I bought a small gold bracelet in a twist design—my favorite. Every day since, when I put it on, I say to myself, "Let go and let God." It's a daily reminder.

Exercise 2-4: Do you have any props to remind you to be the person you truly want to be?

2-5: Thanks

This morning for breakfast I ate a toasted cheese, bacon, and tomato sandwich.

We drive for about thirty minutes, one way, to buy these tomatoes from a Hispanic family with a vegetable stand by the side of the road. Without doubt, they are the best tomatoes I have ever eaten. Once we bought their zucchini that came with advice for how to cook it on the grill. It was the first time Harlan ever liked zucchini.

This morning, with breakfast, I gave thanks for the Hispanic family with a vegetable stand by the side of the road.

Exercise 2-5: At this moment, what do you give thanks for?

2-6: Grace

The invitation was for socially distanced appetizers on our friends' patio in the late afternoon. I expected some cheese and crackers with maybe a few grapes.

Instead, Harlan and I experienced small plate after plate of elegant, fresh hors d'oeuvres from a recipe collection our hostess had been saving for years.

By the end of the evening, I felt that I had been showered with generosity.

Exercise 2-6: Have you experienced treatment that went far beyond in grace and generosity?

2-7: The Energy of Gliding

On a crisp fall morning, after my meditation, I decided to put on some Broadway music and glide through the kitchen. By the time I finished, I had made split pea soup in the slow cooker, six sausage biscuits for Harlan, and two loaves of pumpkin bread.

All this was interspersed with cleaning the refrigerator, stove top, appliances, and counters, as well as unloading the dishwasher, emptying the trash, and changing the sheets on the bed.

It was only 10:00.

This burst of energy was so much fun. Where it came from—the weather, my diet, the music, my meditation with friends, God—I don't know. I do know that I am grateful.

Exercise 2-7: Have you ever had a burst of energy? Have you felt you were gliding through tasks? Tell the story.

2-8: A Christmas Story

My 16-month-old daughter, just before Christmas, contracted spinal meningitis. A vigilant nurse realized she had been misdiagnosed with pneumonia and called the doctor back to the hospital. ASAP. Her action led the doctor to say, "I think we caught the meningitis early enough that there won't be any permanent damage—if she lives."

For 10 long days Anne Marie lay lifeless in an oxygen tent with tubes keeping her fed and medicated. Then, on Christmas Eve, the doctor came in, unhooked all the tubes, and removed the tent. I picked her up and held her close.

The nurse saw the panic on my face when my daughter couldn't hold her head up. Reassuringly, she said, "Don't worry. These little ones recover quickly." She was right--by the end of the day, my precious daughter was running down the hospital hallway.

That night, Christmas Eve, I slept more soundly than I had slept for many days, lying in a hospital bed beside my healthy daughter. Sometime during the night, someone crept in and left a flannel stocking filled with small toys.

Every year I hang a red flannel stocking and give thanks for the doctor and nurses who saved my daughter's life. I pray for the hospitals, doctors, and nurses who are saving others' loved ones right now.

Exercise 2-8: What is your story of an exceptional Christmas gift?

Chapter 3 - Understanding: Gateway to Acceptance

Imagine hot lava from the coast of the Big Island in Hawaii has formed a high arch from the mainland to the sea, as if a gateway.

When I made my first trip to Hawaii, my son had recently been diagnosed with ADHD and alcoholism, two conditions that affect his behavior. Honestly, I had resented some of his past words and behaviors. But with this new information I was able to transform my way of thinking about his past actions and have compassion for both of us.

Now in Hawaii, as I watched the sea foam underneath a lava arch, full realization came that my son is acting in accordance with who he is and what he struggles with, neither of which have anything to do with me. In other words, it's not my fault, and nothing I can say or do will change him. The space in the archway allows each of us to be who we authentically are.

3-1: From Mushiness to Clarity

About a year ago I made a career change. Instead of being a coach who also writes, I decided to be a writer who also coaches.

But I didn't phrase it in such a clear way. Instead, I said, "I'm going to see fewer clients in order to focus on my writing."

Writing has always come easily for me. It's fun, effortless. I even love revision. It doesn't seem like work.

Work has driven me for most of my life. It's been the pressure at my back, the weight on my shoulders. To say writing is work seems strange. It's a new, light sensation. For the last year, I've felt adrift.

I think I'll stop using the word W O R K. If people ask what I do, I'll say, with a light heart, "I'm a writer who also coaches a few people with life and work issues."

This is how change happens for me, from mushiness to clarity. Once I'm clear, the change manifests.

Exercise 3-1: What are you being mushy about? By your mushiness, what change are you delaying?

3-2: Love Encompasses All

I've been thinking about people I know who forgave betrayal and reclaimed their marriages, taking love to a new level.

I have such a strong tendency to decide who's right, who's wrong, what's good and not, separating and segregating the ingredients that compose life.

But the truth is, God loves the soup.

So just for today, I ask my judgmental voice to relax and allow me to savor the flavor of this imperfect, exquisite life.

Exercise 3-2: What is your experience with acceptance?

3-3: Minding My Own Business

For whatever reason, I've felt that if I told people what they're doing wrong and point out how they should change, they would appreciate my wise words, thank me, and make the suggested adjustment.

I hope you're laughing right now at how preposterous and arrogant my thinking has been.

My metamorphosis came in stages. First, I had to learn not to tell people what to do or how to behave. Then I had to accept the fact that my way isn't the only way.

In other words, I had to behave my way into believing. The result is the delicious freedom that comes from minding my own business.

Exercise 3-3: What is your experience with minding your own business?

3-4: Hawks and Illusions

I heard the large bird hit the window, and I shuddered. As I walked to the window, I hoped to see a stunned bird who would soon right himself and fly away.

Instead, I saw a bird on its back, legs up, dead. Quickly, I turned my eyes away. Nearby, a large bluish gray bird I assumed to be his partner watched from the patio wall as Harlan removed the carcass. My heart broke, thinking a pair had been separated by death.

The next morning the same bluish gray bird returned to the patio wall, looking for the missing one. I burst into tears and ran to Harlan. "That bird is back to look for his partner! It makes me so sad."

He said, "Nancy, the bird who died was a quail. This bird you're looking at is a hawk, returning to look for a meal he thought he would get."

His words changed everything. This hawk looked different from those I was familiar with, and I didn't recognize a predator. Oh, my, the stories I can make up in my head!

Exercise 3-4: Are there stories you have made up in your head that you need to share with someone, to get a different perspective?

3-5: The 0.5 Percent

99.5 percent of my life is wonderful. My health and that of my family is good. I have everything I need and most of what I want. Loving, kind relationships prevail.

Except in the 0.5 percent. Especially during holidays, filled with Hallmark movies where love prevails, reconciliation reigns, and gentle snow falls, I start focusing on the 0.5 percent. Old resentments rise up, and the 0.5% seems bigger than the 95.5.

It's during these times that I take longer meditations, focusing on forgiveness and letting go—seeing the beauty of my life and giving thanks—refocusing on the 95.5 percent. I imagine my life as a work of art, with one tiny flaw. Slowly, ever so slowly, the flaw fades and finally disappears.

Exercise 3-5: What we focus on gets stronger. What are you focusing on?

3-6: The Energy of Gifts

Not everyone has my sensitivity, but to me the spirit in which a gift is given is more important than the gift itself. I want my gifts to say, "I honor you and hereby express my love for you."

Some of my greatest disappointments have come when I've given a gift in this spirit with no acknowledgement from the receiver. It isn't good for me to put my heart and soul into a gift and then be ignored. So, with these recipients, I did something different.

I found charities whose missions fit the interest of my recipients and made a donation in their honor. The charities unfailingly thank me for my gift, and my heart is satisfied that I gave something that honors and expresses my love. I send my loved ones a note, so they know. Then I let it go.

Exercise 3-6: Is there any adjustment you would like to make in gift-giving? What is it?

3-7: They Are Not at Fault

Much of our pain begins when we find fault and try to fix or justify what we think is wrong. I've been stuck in that bog for a few weeks.

Last Friday I expressed the desire of my heart to be free of my own judgmentalism. Saturday morning, in an open AA meeting, my answer came when I heard these words in the opening reading: "They are not at fault."

Today this is the mantra I'm living by. If someone is behaving in a way that makes no sense to me, I can just walk on by without trying to figure out what's wrong or attempt to control them with my criticism. I can say to myself, "They are not at fault." I can live in peace.

Exercise 3-7: Where are you "stuck" to your opinion? What is the desire of your heart?

3-8: Simplicity and Consistency

When I opened the car door, loose papers fell out, straying from the seat full of packaging, envelopes, cups, and other objects strewn in no particular order. As my friend quickly gathered and threw them in the back seat to make room for me in the front, she said, "This jumble represents my life right now. I'm a mess."

When we arrived at the coffee shop, I listened for a long while to her flit from topic to topic, telling me what's wrong with her. Finally, she asked me what she should do to make her life more manageable and focused.

"Do these two things every day," I said. "(1) Pray only for knowledge of God's will and the power to carry it out (which is step 11 of recovery programs). (2) Write a short love letter to yourself every day. Do these two things for at least forty days."

We can't make our lives better by fixing everything that's "wrong" with us. But if we strengthen our spiritual core, our lives become manageable. Simplicity and consistency.

Exercise 3-8: Look around. What is your environment saying about you? What would you like to see changed?

3-9: Turbulence

"We are not saints" is a profound statement from the *Big Book of Alcoholics Anonymous.* Indeed, not one of us is. As hard as we might try to do the right thing or to feel calm and centered, occasionally something happens that disturbs our peace.

When disturbance happened to me, first, I felt confused. Then I was angry, with a little hurt mixed in. Then, briefly, the air cleared and I thought the issue was resolved. But no. Wham! Another hit.

I felt like a passenger on a flight experiencing turbulence. A pilot can't see air streams colliding. They are invisible and unavoidable. But, oh my, what fear and injury they are capable of inflicting on passengers and crew when the airplane gets caught in that agitation!

We know what to do if we get caught in turbulence while flying. Keep our seat belts fastened. But what do we do if the turbulence is emotional?

Very much like an airplane pilot, I got out of the turbulence as quickly as was feasible, with a goal of the least injury possible. The most difficult part of the process for me was moving away from my own anger and blame, replacing it with acceptance. Acceptance is a neutral emotion—a much kinder place to be. A seat belt, if you will.

Exercise 3-9: Have you experienced any turbulence? What did you do?

3-10: Harmony with All That Is

> Acceptance is a rubber raft,
> Floating, with me in it.
> I pass by limbs,
> Rocks, underbrush on the bank,
> Easing safely through
> Debris and distraction from beauty.
> I slip into the day in
> Harmony with all that is.

Exercise 3-10: What is harmony to you?

3-11: Sometimes a Moment

> Sometimes a moment comes
> When all my yesterdays
> Line up in perfect formation
> And I understand.

Exercise 3-11: Is anything in your life nagging at you, unresolved and maybe even resented? Write or draw it and put it in a "God box" until the day it is ready to be woven into the fabric of your life, and you see it clearly for what it is.

3-12: The Mirror

In *Hamlet*, Shakespeare wrote that one purpose of theatre is "to hold the mirror ...up to nature." In other words, it helps us see ourselves as others see us.

A few days ago, I heard myself say, "You're gonna love it!" as if I can force another person's response. Then I realized the phrase sounded familiar. I won't be saying that again.

I view politics as drama—an opportunity to glimpse the best and worst within myself. I leave others to do as they will.

Exercise 3-12: How do you view the current political scene? How might you use it to make you better?

3-13: Reminders from a Jigsaw Puzzle

A friend lent me a wooden jigsaw puzzle, the first I had ever seen. It is an elegant creation with beautiful, interesting pieces of unusual shapes. Challenging and fun, working it reminded me of several important truths:

- I find what I'm looking for when I'm looking for something else.
- I do best when I relax and let the puzzle work itself.
- A good light helps me see subtle differences. Not everything belongs where I think it does.
- Telling myself what I should be able to do doesn't help.
- It's best to work on small bits until it's clear how they fit the bigger picture.
- Just as I become convinced there are missing pieces, it all falls into place.
- I must be oh, so gentle.

Exercise 3-13: What lessons have you learned or re-learned from observing yourself in your daily life?

3-14: What Counts

I no longer earn a salary and define my worth through professional accomplishments. How shall I measure my worth?

I've been feeling as if I'm aimlessly drifting. Then I had a conversation with my dear cousin, who has been retired for many years. I asked, "What do you do with your time?" She said, "Oh, I'm so busy! I walk five miles a day. I take care of my home, and there's always lots to do. Yesterday I planted flowers in the front bed."

To myself I thought, "That counts?!" Then I realized, "Yes. That counts."

When I'm kind and affirming to Harlan, that counts. If I clean the outdoor grill, that counts. If I have a heart-to-heart talk with a friend, that counts. If I text my children to have a good day, that counts.

Starting today, I will count living well as worthy, fulfilling accomplishment.

Exercise 3-14: How do you measure your worth?

3-15: Helpers Come

I used to believe that I had to do everything all by myself, making life more stressful than it truly is. I could not accept aid or comfort.

Along the way, I changed. I came to realize that I just couldn't go it alone any longer, and I started accepting help. I changed a lifelong pattern.

Last week our precious dog Teddy had surgery for a torn ACL, and when I saw his condition after surgery, I was heartbroken and anxious. In the night, as I held him close to comfort him, he lifted his paw for me to rub his tummy—the first sign that the Teddy I love was still there. I started to breathe.

Early the next morning, texts of encouragement started to ping my phone, the first one from a friend who didn't even know what I was going through.

Exercise 3-15: When have helpers come for you? What help would you like right now?

3-16: What We Need Is Provided

Several years ago, Harlan and I went to Cyprus. It was an amazing trip, full of discoveries and surprises. One of those surprises was no washcloths in the hotel bathroom. Towels, yes. Washcloths, no.

The first day we walked along the Mediterranean, with shops and restaurants and street vendors, one of whom was selling sponges harvested from the sea. Of course, I bought one to serve as a washcloth! Ever since, that sponge has rested on the corner of my bathtub. I haven't used it since Cyprus.

Last week, noticing how dry the sponge was, I threw it away with the realization that what I need continues to be provided. I don't have to hold onto that sponge.

Exercise 3-16: Are you clinging to something that worked in the past but is no longer needed? What is it?

3-17: Breath

> Islands disappear—reappear.
> Tides come in and go out.
> Neighbors move.
> Children grow, leave, and
> Return—maybe—to visit.
> Friends die.
> Breath moves through all of it.

Inhaling—exhaling—
Inhaling—exhaling—

Exercise 3-17: What remains constant for you through all of life's changes?

3-18: The Big Shift

I used to measure the success of my day by how much I got done—how many tasks I listed and checked off on my calendar.

In the last few years I've made a focused effort to pay attention to the energy I put into each day, not the activity. Am I being kind? Am I being guided by love? Am I being true to my authentic self? Do I respect and accept others? Have I allowed my emotions to be hijacked by the latest news or catastrophe or someone else's behavior? In the end, we all come to the end. What matters is how we lived, not what we did.

Exercise 3-18: How do you measure success?

3-19: It's Always a Choice

Just now I promised myself that this Thanksgiving week will be simple, easy, and joyful.

We are having family and friends for dinner on Thursday. I'm focused on relaxing and putting our guests at ease.

Today I'll receive a large shipment of pecans to be distributed to friends and P.E.O. sisters. I've made a decision to slip this effort into my Thanksgiving preparations seamlessly.

Chaos wants to rule—to hijack me emotionally and make me anxious and irritable. But I choose peace.

Always, it's a choice.

Exercise 3-19: What state of mind do you choose today?

3-20: Humility

Science writer David Blatner affirms that there are more stars in the universe than grains of sand on earth. Moreover, he writes that in just ten drops of water, the number of molecules exceeds the number of stars in the universe. Reading his words makes me realize that so much is beyond my comprehension, and if I try to figure it out, I'm likely to be wrong. Thus, I arrive at humility—learning to be content when I don't know and can't figure it out.

Exercise 3-20: What realization brings you to humility?

3-21: Getting Out of a Funk

Yesterday I was in a funk. I knew it had to do with food, but I could not articulate more specifically what my problem was.

This morning I decided to journal to discover the essence of the funk. Surprisingly, here's what I wrote: "Cooking is Mother's job. I'm not Mother, and she's not here."

At first, as I read what I had written, I thought, "Oh. This funk is connected to grief." No. Instead, it's not wanting to repeat my mother's food behavior and not knowing what to do. It's anger that I must change.

Last week I started asking people like me what they do about food preparation. One of them said she has about ten simple, healthy meal plans that she alternates. That sounds like something I can do. So today I begin a new approach, and I think my funk will dissipate.

Exercise 3-21: Has anything been nagging at you? Have you tried journaling to discover the source?

3-22: Faith

Harlan and I went to a performance by Jim Curry, who looks and sounds remarkably like the late John Denver.

The performance included visuals, one of which was an eagle taking flight. As I watched, that eagle simply spread his wings and allowed the invisible air current to lift him.

In that moment I realized what faith is.

Exercise 3-22: What image comes to mind when you think of faith?

3-23: Forgive Us Our Trespasses

The late James G. Prator, my friend's father, received his theology degree late in life, after two careers. He loved to translate the Bible from the language in which it was written. Here is his translation of the portion of the Lord's Prayer that we know as, "Forgive us our trespasses as we forgive those who trespass against us:"

> "Untie the tangled threads of destiny that bind and imprison us, as we release others from their mistakes and errors of judgment."

Exercise 3-23: How would your life be different if you "release[d] others from their mistakes and errors of judgment"?

3-24: Don't Let the Old Man In

Country music star Toby Keith and legendary actor Clint Eastwood were conversing. Eastwood said that the following week, he would begin shooting another movie.

With reference to the fact that Eastwood is in his 80's, Keith asked, "How do you do it?"

Eastwood, with his characteristic grin, replied, "When I get up in the morning, I don't let the old man in." Subsequently, Eastwood wrote a song with that title.

Author and concentration camp survivor Viktor Frankl in his book *Man's Search for Meaning* wrote that, despite circumstances, we have the ability to decide what we allow into our minds. How we begin our day determines to a great extent the kind of day we will have. We decide what can come into our consciousness. The good news is that, if we sense that we are going in the wrong direction, we can begin our day over—any time.

Exercise 3-24: How did your day begin?

3-25: The Gift of Acceptance

At a time when I felt forlorn, I received a gift in a daughter's letter—someone else's daughter, yet my own. Her simple, eloquent words said, "Thank you for helping me find my way to restore my faith in me."

Her gift to me was accepting what I had to give.

Exercise 3-25: When has someone given you the gift of accepting what you offered?

3-26: Will to Be Whole

Fragmentation was what I learned growing up and through much of my adulthood. First do this; now do that, with no connection between the two.

For a friend, I set an intention to have the "will to be whole." Then I realized this is a prayer for myself, too. Life truly is a flow, not a collection of tasks. If I stay in the center of love, things work out, effortlessly.

Today may you have the will to be whole.

Exercise 3-26: How do these words ring true for you?

3-27: You Can't Make a Mistake

I was sanding a bowl I had made in pottery class, preparing it to be bisqued. A chunk of the side came off in my hand, and I was heading towards the trash with it when the instructor stopped me. "What are you doing with that?"

"I'm throwing it away," I responded. "I broke it."

"No, no," he said. "That opening is a perfect big spoon rest for when you're cooking. See? The handle goes right here," and he pointed to the hole I had made. "In here there are no mistakes."

Exercise 3-27: What would you do if you knew you couldn't make a mistake?

3-28: Who Do I Want to Be?

A young woman shared that her mother, in a phone call, had attacked her with expletives. The daughter said," The last time this happened, I didn't speak to her for fifteen years. But this time I decided to do it differently. I thought to myself, "Regardless of her behavior, who do I want to be?"

It's easy to react to someone else's unacceptable behavior, but the higher road is being who we truly want to be, no matter what.

Exercise 3-28: Who is it that you truly want to be, no matter what?

3-29: A Channel for Grace

Images of gold have been coming to me, first in the words my friend Ash Almonte, artist for this book's cover, assigned to a figurative painting of a woman. These are lyrics Ash chose for her work from "The Difference in the Shades" by Bright Eyes: "But these are the days we dream about, when the sunlight paints us gold."

These words piqued my interest in gold, and I learned that it is one of the least reactive chemical elements—that it is soft, malleable, and pliable. It's found in nuggets, in rocks, in veins, in river deposits.

To me, gold is like grace—the influence or spirit of God operating in humans. My prayer today is to make me a channel for grace.

Exercise 3-29: What does gold symbolize to you?

3-30: Kindness and Respect

Instead of a resolution this year, I simply made a commitment to kindness and respect. To be sure I knew what I was committing to, I looked up both words.

Kindness comes from the heart. It requires empathy and giving love and consideration to others.

Respect is due regard for the feelings, wishes, rights, or traditions of others.

Giving kindness and respect doesn't take anything away from me. It doesn't mean being a doormat. Rather, it encourages my heart. The gift gives both ways. What I give to others comes back to me.

Exercise 3-30: What experience have you had with a two-way gift?

3-31: Something New

When I started working with clay, I quickly learned that I prefer hand building to the wheel. I've also learned

- There isn't just one right way to work with clay.
- My teachers and fellow classmates are friendly and eager to share.
- It's okay to throw out something that didn't work.
- Inspiration will eventually come.
- A creative glaze can mask flaws.
- Even if I think I'm copying, what I make with my hands is original.

- It's really just mud.

Exercise 3-31: Have you tried something new that stretched you? What did you learn?

3-32: Opportunity

The coronavirus pandemic gave me the opportunity to spend more time at home—to cook, work a wooden puzzle, read, take a walk, do a bit of yard work. It's also giving me the impetus for reflection—to take a look at what's around me and ask if there's anything I want to change that would improve the quality of my life.

When I asked myself this question, the answer that came was, "Sheets. Get rid of those sheets." They are very nice sheets, but I don't like the way they feel, and the top sheet is really too big even for our king-size bed.

Some things we tend to tolerate because they aren't worn out or someone we love gave them to us—or "they are very nice sheets." Since we're all being reminded of how fragile our lives are, this is a good time to improve its quality.

Exercise 3-32: What are you tolerating? How might your energy improve if it weren't there?

3-33: In All Things

An old friend mocked me for living such a privileged life that it is easy for me to live in meditative gratitude. Since he spoke, I've carefully considered what he said. Is gratitude only for the well-off? I think not.

My grandmother was poor, with only a third-grade education. Yet, she was grateful for her life and her family. I've read, "In all things, give thanks." Also, I know that gratitude is good for the human system, even boosting immunity. It's good for all people, regardless of circumstance.

Today's headlines are scary. Our life experiences have been altered. Still, the gambrel quail run across the yard, for anyone with eyes to see. The run rises, shines, and then sets. Spring's pink and yellow blooms burst forth. This morning's moon was a beautiful sliver. We have enough food. We have our health. Regardless of what happens tomorrow, I choose to live in gratitude today.

Exercise 3-33: In these days, what is your choice?

3-34: What's Right for Me

When I was growing up, Mother used to say, "Just because someone else is doing it, doesn't make it right for you."

Now I know that peer pressure isn't just a teenage phenomenon. It never leaves; it just gets more subtle.

In these days of no contact with peers, I've been asking, "What's right for me? When these days are over, what will I pick up again, and what will I let go?"

Because of digestive issues, so I did an inventory of what my body needs and what it doesn't tolerate well. I researched what works to alleviate my distress. I didn't consider TV commercials or diet/exercise programs or foods that Harlan likes. I simply asked, "What is my body telling me? What loving response am I ready to make?"

Yesterday I began making some adjustments, and I have a pathway going forward that's right for me.

Exercise 3-34:What's your experience with peer pressure?

3-35: Let Life Be Life

I often sit on our patio in the morning, watching and listening to the birds and enjoying the amazing scenery.

This morning I noticed the loud "caw, caw, caw" of a raven diving at a juniper tree. Obviously, there was a nest in the tree, probably full of eggs because that's what ravens love to eat.

In a moment, there were three ravens. Then five. Finally, I counted ten, all cawing and diving at the top of that tree. Finally, they started to disperse, one at a time, until there were none.

Did the smaller birds successfully protect the nest? Or did the ravens take all the eggs? I do not know. The drama brought to my mind this slogan: "Let life be life." In either event, all is well with me.

Exercise 3-35: When have you let life be life?

3-36: Accepting What I Cannot Change

This weekend tourists came back to Sedona in droves without masks.

What this means to me is stay home. Wait for them to leave. Take precautions when I go out. Be patient. This, too, shall pass.

When things I don't like, happen, I have choices. I can write a letter to the editor or post a rant on Next Door or call someone to complain. But honestly, I'm tired of reactivity.

I choose to be grateful that, for our merchants, business has picked up. Then I do what is needed to take care of myself.

Many years ago, I learned that what I focus on gets stronger. I choose peace.

Exerckse 3-36: What's your experience with accepting things you cannot change?

3-37: Divinity

To be present, in a way, at my brother/sister/niece's Thanksgiving, I decided to make a batch of divinity, a white homemade fudge, and mail it to them to enjoy during the visit. When Harlan heard my plans, he insisted I make two batches, one for him.

The first batch, try as I might, would not harden. Finally, after beating and beating and beating, I gave up and poured it into a buttered Pyrex pan. I set the pan aside and then began the second batch, thinking Harlan would just have to eat his candy with a spoon.

The second batch turned out well, hardened easily. I packed it, addressed the package, and took it to the Post Office. After I returned home, I mustered the courage to check on the first batch. Unbelievably, it felt firm to my touch. Then I sliced it into cubes of delicious divinity. No spoons required.

Why am I telling you this? Because every now and then something happens to bring home the truth that when I stop beating, let go, and let God, miracles happen.

Exercise 3-37: When do miracles happen for you?

Chapter 4 - Be Joyful

Imagine a dolphin breaking through the water to the surface of the blue Caribbean Sea, splashing up onto its tail, enjoying the moment.

Vividly do I remember the first time I experienced joy. I was driving past Mount Bonnell in Austin, Texas. I stopped the car, to appreciate the spectacular view of Lake Austin and the edge of the Hill Country. When I turned back to the wheel, I felt an unfamiliar, ecstatic sensation. Something within said, "That's joy." Thus, I learned that joy is in the moment, when I am open to it.

4-1: Incrementally Better

What I want is to be dazzlingly perfect the first time I try something, check that off my list, and move on.

I've been playing games on an app designed to keep the brain agile. One particular game irritates me because I cannot get a perfect score. Each time I get slightly better, the game gets harder.

This morning I looked back at my scores and realized that all along, I've gotten incrementally better. I also realized I'll never conquer it.

Then I realized that all that is truly important to me has been gained through steady, daily effort that results in tiny, incremental shifts, not conquest:

- A peaceful, joyful spiritual life through daily practice
- A happy marriage through a daily decision to be loving and forgiving
- Good family relations through constantly letting go
- Friendships through showing up and being real
- Pain-free knees and shoulders, thanks to physical therapy and daily exercise
- Improved health through being honest about what I eat and how much I move

Remember the fable of the tortoise and the hare? Steady wins the race.

In Goethe's words, "Whatever you can do or dream you can, begin it. Boldness had genius and magic in it."

Exercise 4-1: What are you ready to begin and stick with?

4-2: Rewrite the Script

When we are young, we learn patterns of thinking and feeling that, unless we intervene, can direct the rest of our lives.

One of my old scripts was that I didn't get the emotional support and encouragement I needed from my mother, so it was difficult for me to trust women and I had few female friends.

Then one day I wrote about all the women who had helped and encouraged me along the way: a neighbor, a teacher, a church leader, a boss, a colleague. I was getting what I needed all along. Then I began to appreciate all that my mother had actually done for me.

Thus, I rewrote my script. Today I have many female friends, and I've learned to trust women. I've also learned to meet my own emotional needs. Friends simply enrich my life.

Exercise 4-2: What old script would you like to rewrite? Where will you begin?

4-3: A Good Day

Rains have plunged the temperature into jacket weather. The leaves of the cottonwood are beginning to turn yellow, like their cousin the aspen. The crisp coolness and clear, bright air give new life to my spirit.

I had already put my beautiful glass pumpkins on the table in the entry to our home and adorned the dining table with an autumn arrangement—reminders that the seasons are shifting.

Then I bought a red clay pumpkin whose goofy grin greets me every morning from his perch on the patio, visible from my bed.

How could I not have a good day?

Exercise 4-3: What gives you a good day?

4-4: Dawdling

Some of my happiest times are when I'm dawdling. The way it works for me is that as I move through my day, if something gets my attention, I attend to it right away.

During my last dawdling period, I sat to pet the dogs as long as they wanted. I clipped the loose threads on the table runner I bought on our trip to San Miguel de Allende. I put out the pumpkin plate for display.

If I force myself to keep the schedule I've made and disallow dawdling, my thoughts of what's undone begin to mount in my brain, and I eventually become anxious or stressed. It's so much better if I do those small tasks as I recognize them.

I don't believe this phenomenon is unique to me. I've noticed that my daughter's voice on the phone is happiest when she has a day to meander, walk, stop in her favorite shops, sit in the chair with a cat in her lap, or lounge in her beautiful back yard with a coffee.

Dawdling clears my heart and mind.

Exercise 4-4: What clears your heart and mind? When was the last time you did it?

4-5: A Perfect Day

Someone asked me once what is my idea of a perfect day. At the time, I gave an answer that was mostly about the activity I had packed into the day. But since, I have realized that a perfect day is one in which my heart is simply filled with gratitude. Like today.

Snow is falling as I write. Not the kind that snarls traffic and complicates life, but gentle snowflakes falling softly to the ground and melting. I'm grateful for the beauty and peace of it.

Harlan and I had our favorite breakfast at a nearby restaurant. We sat next to a couple from San Antonio. When they left, a couple from Arkansas took their table. I'm grateful to live in a place where I meet and converse with interesting tourists who appreciate the beauty of Sedona and want to hear our stories of what it's like to live here.

I'm grateful for a day when I can simply stay in a warm house, watch the birds feeding from the seed I just left outside, and do what I feel like doing, from one moment to the next. A perfect day.

Exercise 4-5: What is a perfect day for you?

4-6: Savor

> We sat, my friend and I,
> At a table spread with
> Bits of cheese and chocolate,
> Apple bites and crackers,
> Lettuce and tomato.
> Slowly we ate, noticing
> The subtle differences,
> Focusing on the gift of food
> And friendship.
> Thus, I learned to savor.

Note: This experience was with a high school classmate who now lives in Cairo, Egypt. She came to visit me in Sedona with her amazing chocolates, and together we created this array from what I had on hand.

Exercise 4-6: When was the last time you savored something? What was it like?

4-7: Do It Now, Or It Doesn't Matter

> In my perfectionistic mind,
> Energy sticks, trapped,
> When I look out and see imperfection.
> I think, you see, that I can fix it.
> To restore my sanity,
> I have adopted a new mantra:
> Do it now, or it doesn't matter.

Exercise 4-7: How do you notice energy getting stuck in your mind? What new mantra might release it?

4-8: Rewriting the Script

> Someone wrote a script for me.

Go to school.
Marry.
Raise children.
Have a good career.
The script stopped there.
So, I had to rewrite the script
To learn to be happy in a new marriage—
To live my life easily and joyfully—
To work for purpose and calling.
Now is a new phase of my life—
The last one? Maybe.
I'm looking for the trail to walk
That enfolds and infuses me
With perfect peace and bursts of joy.

Exercise 4-8: What is the script of your life? Where are you now?

4-9: Unexpected Gift

Harlan and I removed a large round manzanita bush to open up the view of the red rocks from our terrace. I was a bit sad about our decision to have it removed because it was a beautifully shaped bush, and in bloom. But it was in the wrong place.

The next morning, early, as I sat in bed, I looked out the bedroom window to see a new scene. A pond at the bottom of the hill with ducks skimming the surface in duck play. Beyond, the village nestled at the base of the hills, awakening in the early morning sun, its rays bringing adobe houses to life.

We knew the manzanita removal would open up the view of the rocks from the terrace, but we had no idea of the new view from our bedroom. It was an unexpected gift.

Exercise 4-9: When have you taken action that resulted in an unexpected gift?

4-10: What's Your Dream?

On the other side of the dream is the stuff of other dreams. We dream it—live it—then dream again, in a pattern that weaves our lives.

Exercise 4-10: How have dreams led you through your life? How have your dreams changed? What is your dream right now?

4-11: Let's Play

After a long day of driving, Harlan and I went to dinner at a pub with lots of games. We chose table shuffleboard, which I won. On our way back to the hotel, we passed a miniature golf course, made a u-turn, and played eighteen holes.

It lifted our spirits to play.

Exercise 4-11: When was the last time you spontaneously played?

4-12: Ride the Current of Love

A friend told me about challenges of being a mother of young children, a wife, and an artist. To meet all of her obligations, she had made a schedule for her day: Get up at 4:30 a.m., get to the gym by 5:00, go back home and paint until the children awaken.

The only problem with the schedule was that the baby didn't follow it. He started waking up every morning at 2:30 and then again at 4:30. My friend was tired and also frustrated that she couldn't follow the schedule she had so meticulously made.

My advice to her (which she had asked for) was, "Throw away the schedule; instead, list priorities and then dance with them." She identified these priorities:

1. Self-care, including time every day for meditation and communicating with God.

2. Spouse's well-being. Take care of the marriage and give it what it needs.

3. Children's well-being. Make sure they get time for play with you and being outside together, as well as the routine care.

4. Create art.

Only four things to remember. Ride the current of love throughout your day. Set priorities and then dance with them. Relax and enjoy.

Exercise 4-12: How well are you dancing with your life right now?

4-13: Blessing

May you be infused with peace. May you find joy. May good health make your life enjoyable. May you laugh and be at ease. May you be surrounded by people who love you.

Exercise 4-13: What blessing would you like to send today to everyone you meet?

4-14: Carefree

I awoke with the word "carefree" on my mind, so I looked it up. One definition is "not holding onto worries or resentments." In other words, letting go.

Letting go is something I've been learning for many years. These days, most of the time, my peace is not disturbed by events beyond my control or other people's behavior.

In her poem "She Let Go," Safire Rose wrote, "Like a leaf falling from a tree, she just let go." This sentence so resonates with me that I wrote it on the front page of my journal, as a daily reminder.

In that moment of letting go, the leaf does not remember the limitations of being connected to the tree or feel the fear of falling. It's carefree.

Exercise 4-14: What is your experience of being carefree?

4-15: Find the Joy in Every Day

In a meditation at the Saint Louis Basilica, these words came to me: "Find the joy in every day."

This day, already I have found joy. First, in folding the sheets—a simple, ordinary task; then, on a hike when Harlan pointed out a century plant, blooming yellow/white.

"Find the joy in every day" is now my mantra. The joy is there. My job is to see it and to pay attention when others point it out.

Exercise 4-15: Where do you find joy?

4-16: The World I Choose to Live In

My across-the-fence neighbor gave me a half bushel of lemons from a tree in her Phoenix backyard. Then my around-the-corner neighbor brought a batch of delicious apricots. Finally, my down-the-street neighbor asked us to pick all the blackberries we wanted—enough for two cobblers!

At a baseball game, a young man in front of me caught a ball. Then he turned around and tossed it to a handicapped teen sitting two rows behind him.

In my world, love and neighborliness abound.

Exercise 4-16: How does neighborliness show up in your world?

4-17: What's Inside My Hula Hoop

A good question for me to ask, when I feel despair and consternation over events beyond my control, is, "What's inside my hula hoop?" That question restores my focus and keeps me away from that which is beyond me.

Today I'm learning to work wooden jigsaw puzzles. Not cardboard. Wooden. Puzzles that can't be worked by setting the border first. Puzzles with whimsey pieces that go together in unusual ways. Puzzles that challenge my brain not to follow the same, timeworn route, but to imagine new possibilities.

Exercise 4-17: What are you doing to open new possibilities?

4-18: Adjusting Expectations

Much of our unhappiness or disappointment begins when we set an expectation. I've spent the last eight months planning a trip to Yellowknife and Banff, Canada, with my daughter and daughter-in-law. The original reason for going was to see the aurora borealis, and our information was that our chances were 97% at the time of year we planned to go.

On the morning we were to take the aurora tour, I checked the forecast. Only a 40% chance of seeing the northern lights.

Momentarily, I was disappointed. But then, I realized no one knows for sure when these magical lights will appear. Besides, I will be in new surroundings with two people I love, seeing beauty and experiencing wonder. What could be better than that?

P.S. The lights did appear. They were white, not green or purple, but amazing and magical.

Exercise 4-18: What is your experience with setting expectations?

4-19: Tiny Gifts

My heart is being filled with the joy of giving tiny gifts: a tea bag holder I made in pottery class and wrapped in a cellophane bag with three or four bags of special tea or a few pieces of homemade divinity fudge wrapped in plastic and tied with a small bow.

Exercise 4-19: Right now, what is bringing you joy?

Chapter 5 - Truth Simply Stands

Imagine a saguaro cactus standing alone in a desert landscape, blue sky with wispy white clouds as a backdrop.

Saguaros live 150-200 years, so a tall saguaro against a desert sky holds the wisdom of life through all those years. It has nothing to say. It simply stands.

5-1: Transformation

Growing up, my daughter was quiet and sky. She relied on other people to speak for her in social situations. As she grew older, she had difficulty moving into adulthood.

On a visit with her, I realized what an independent, strong woman she has become. What created the transformation? You'll have to ask her; that's her story.

My observation is that she moved to a city she loves, far away from everyone she knew. She bought a house in the section of that city that perfectly fits the lifestyle she wants. She kept changing jobs until she found one that suits her innate abilities, unique skills, and educational preparation. For many years she has been in a relationship with someone who loves, supports, appreciates, and takes pride in her. They live with two entertaining cats whom they adore, and they live within their means. They treasure their friends and neighbors.

In short, today she is confident and happy. What more could a mother want for her child?

Exercise 5-1: What gives you confidence, strength, happiness, and contentment?

5-2: Let It Be

Lyrics from a Beatles' song have been floating through my head: "Let it be. Let it be. Let it be. Let it be. There will be an answer. Let it be."

So much of my life has been devoted to trying to fix things that weren't the way I thought they should be. This innate, strong tendency makes me look around for something to improve. Isn't that, after all, how progress gets made?

Yet I've learned that when I exert force, resistance is the inevitable result. I may prevail, but only after much exertion and maybe even exhaustion.

This principle is especially true in relationships. Let it be. Give people the freedom and respect to learn what they need to learn when they need to learn it.

Let it be.

Exercise 5-2: What do you need to let be?

5-3: New Standards

In the past, I've measured my success by what and how much I got done. As time has gone by, I've chosen new standards. At the end of the day, I ask myself:

- Did I reach out to call or visit with a friend? Or make a new one?

- Was I respectful of myself and others, even those with whom I disagree?

- Did I treat myself well with diet, rest, exercise, and spiritual practice?

- Did I challenge my mind through reading or other new learning?
- Was I kind, calm, and loving?
- Did I do something just for fun?
- Did I set good boundaries, focusing on what is my business and letting everything else go?

Exercise 5-3 At the end of the day, how do you measure your success?

5-4: Be True

Once I wrapped a finger-shaped crystal with bubble wrap and then stuck small fishhooks all over the outside of the bubble wrap. I did this to illustrate that in the heart of us is purity, where Light lives. But that Light gets blocked by what we wrap around and allow to hook us. These hooks make us behave in ways that mask the truth of who we are.

Do you know what your hooks are? Whatever pulls you out of being the person you truly are—the one you want to be—the one that makes you happiest—is a hook.

Sometimes being true to myself is uncomfortable. It makes me face unpleasantness, be honest, and take action. It might make others uncomfortable. Sometimes it means I won't be doing what everyone else is doing. But oh, the exhilaration that follows as I realize I've been true to myself!

Maybe, just for today, you could slip out of the bubble wrap and simply be true to yourself.

Exercise 5-4: What will you do today that is true to yourself?

5-5: Compassion in Controversy

The life of a new friend spins around controversy. Each time we meet, it seems, her family is in crisis—or her church—or something in the news has triggered her outrage.

I've tried several different responses. I've listened and shared a personal story. Once in a text exchange, I simply wrote, "I have no opinion." She responded, "Seriously??!!" She couldn't imagine it.

I decided to take a different approach by calmly explaining where I stand on a particular issue without casting stones at anyone. I stood for my belief but not against anyone. So far, that approach has worked best.

What I'm searching for is compassion for someone who seems to thrive on dissension. Honestly, I don't like controversy. I ask myself, "How important is it?" In most cases, the answer is, "Not important at all," and I let it go.

But this new friend is challenging me to this opportunity to learn compassion for those who seek controversy.

Exercise 5-5: What is your relationship with controversy?

5-6: The Gift of Authenticity

"Let the inner man and the outer man be one" is how Socrates said it. Today we call it authenticity. Being real. Living to the highest within us. Being true to our best selves.

A gift of authenticity was given by Denise, whom I had just met. She had offered her home in San Miguel de Allende to guests for a mutual friend's wedding. Happily, Harlan and I were invited to be one of only a few people to stay in this beautiful home in the old city, only a few blocks and easy walk to the hotel where the wedding occurred.

In this home, peace prevailed. It wasn't just the layout or the artwork or the lush plants in the fountained courtyard. It was the authenticity of the owner.

Our host realized during the wedding festivities that she wasn't feeling well, so she left the wedding early to go to bed, where she stayed. The last night we were there, she felt well enough to join us for diner. We found some leftover quiche that we had bought a couple of days before in the market. To that, we added some greens and peppers and tomatoes that she had in the refrigerator. For dessert, we sliced some fresh peaches and grapes that we had just bought on the street, combining them with the apples we found in the refrigerator for a dessert fruit salad. We enjoyed conversation over this simple, uncomplicated, elegant meal.

The entire time we were there, we felt free to do what was right for us, with no obligations or expectations, no pretense or orchestration. Peace is the simple gift of authenticity.

Exercise 5-6: When have you received the gift of authenticity? When have you given it?

5-7: The Freedom of Knowing Your Character Defects

Our character defects, no matter what you call them, stick to us through the power of their emotional energy. When we shift the energy to a more desirable state of mind, the defect loosens its grip.

Once when I was eating in a restaurant with friends, the water I had ordered was slow to be delivered. To my tablemates, I said something like, "Where's my water?" One of my friends, laughing, said, "They must not know who you are!"

I laughed as I realized what I was doing, as humility replaced indignation.

I work with some people who say, "Oh, let's not be hard on ourselves. No need to talk about character defects. Could we call them something else?"

When we name it and accept it, it loses its control over us. Then and only then are we free to laugh at ourselves and make different choices.

Exercise 5-7: When was the last time you felt ill at ease? What character defect was rearing its ugly head?

5-8: Attitude Change

I used to believe that spider webs in a house signaled filth and neglect. Then I moved to my current home. Tiny spiders breed in a nearby pond and then make their way into my home. They are so numerous that monthly, we exterminate for spiders!

As the morning sun shines through my bedroom window, I see a glistening spider web in the door frame that I cleaned two days ago.

My attitude towards spider webs has changed. They are not a sign of filth. They are persistent, ingenious creations of silent, invisible artists.

Exercise 5-8: Have you experienced an attitude change? What was it?

5-9: Faith

> Make me an embryo,
> Growing towards grace.
> Not striving. Just letting be.
> Floating, effortlessly.
> This is my prayer.

Exercise 5-9: What is your prayer today?

5-10: Wordless Sharing

I live among the red rocks of Sedona, Arizona. People come here from all over the world to experience the unique beauty. When I hike the trails, I see them stopped on the trail, camera in hand, mouth agape.

"Stunning, isn't it?" I've often said to them. Or "Isn't it gorgeous?" or "What an incredible view!"

Having been here awhile, I have run out of words to describe the phenomenon of nature that surrounds me. No word is sufficient.

So now when I pass tourists on the trail, I pass in silence. I know what they are feeling. I feel it, too. I am content with wordless sharing.

Exercise 5-10: When have you used words when silence is really what is called for?

5-11: Practicing Presence

Red Rock Pathway is my favorite trail, an easy one with spectacular views. I've noticed that I cannot hike and view at the same time. The trail is irregular, strewn with rocks. Overnight, a branch can fall and shatter in a place that was clear yesterday. To be safe, if I'm walking, my eyes are down.

Occasionally, I stop to stand in awe of the spectacular view. But I don't walk and sightsee at the same time.

This observation made me realize what is meant by "presence." When I walk, I'm present for walking. When I stop, I'm present for viewing. My hikes are good practice for life. When Harlan speaks, I want to be present for what he says, not thinking about loading the dishwasher. When I load the dishwasher, I want to be present for dishes.

Exercise 5-11: What do you want to be present for today?

5-12: Native Language

My native language is poetry. As a child, I shut the door to my room and read aloud—even memorized—poems from my mother's high school literature textbook. Many years later, while typing my journal entries into the computer, I was stunned to realize that I had written poetry! A friend is encouraging me to write poetry again. So here goes:

> On this day the cottonwood seeds
> Fly through the air like angels.
> A friend will tell her children
> That she is divorcing their dad.
> Tired travelers go to the airport, inspired after their
> First look at the Grand Canyon and Sedona.
> Another friend grieves
> The death of her dog.

I am happiest and most content when I let my voice speak poetry.

Exercise 5-12: What is your native language? When are you happiest and most content?

5-13: Speak the Truth in Love

It's difficult to speak the truth in love, but that's what fulfills us. We must say what we truly need to say without judgment or condemnation. This is the ultimate form of respect, both for ourselves and for others.

Exercise 5-13: What do you truly need to say?

5-14: Speak Your Truth Quietly and Clearly

In my mother's home hung a framed quotation by Max Ehrmann, a 1927 poem called "Desiderata." A portion goes like this: "Speak your truth quietly and clearly; and listen to others, even the dull and the ignorant; they too have their story."

What reminded me of this quotation was a friend in my book club. In our last meeting, we discussed a book that several women in the group did not like, and they were harsh in their criticism. My friend sat quietly, listening to their comments. Then she said, "I had a different experience from many of you. Here's what I liked and appreciated about this book." She explained without arguing. She didn't try to convince anyone or justify her position. She spoke her truth clearly, simply and quietly and then went silent.

Exercise 5-14: What do you do when you are with people you disagree with?

5-15: Acceptance

My friend owned a car wash in a nearby city. One below-freezing winter morning, she was at work early, catching up on some paperwork. She heard the sprinklers in the self-wash go off. A few minutes later, an angry customer was standing in front of her, furious because now his car with coated with ice. Calmly, she said, "Water freezes at 32 degrees Fahrenheit, and there's nothing I can do about it."

My friend was talking about acceptance. Some people have difficulty even accepting laws of nature. Others of us struggle to change the behavioral set point of others. We think they should be different. We believe they could choose better behavior. We're angry or disappointed when they don't do what we want.

Exercise 5-14: What are you struggling to accept?

5-16: The Energy of Words

In his book *Power vs. Force*, David Hawkins relates that the emotion inherent in the words we read, hear, and say actually weaken or strengthen us, and the effect is measurable. Some words inspire us, lift us, and make us better people. Other words discourage us, anger us, and make us less than who we truly are.

That words have power is the premise of the first agreement Miguel Ruiz writes about in his book *The Four Agreements*. He writes, "Your word is the power that you have to create.... What you dream, what you feel, and what you really are, will all be manifested through the word.... The word is a force; it is the power you have to express and communicate, to think, and thereby to create the events in your life.... Depending on how it is used, the word can set you free, or it can enslave you even more than you know.

Exercise 5-16: Think of the last time your own words made you uneasy. Think of the last time your own words made you feel fulfilled. Just write or draw the story.

5-17: Speak the Truth in Love

Acting from love in all interactions is ideal, but what about really difficult situations?

It is our tone that reveals our true meaning. It reveals the feeling behind our words. It is the energy of the emotion that people react to, not the words.

Try this experiment: For the next week, pay attention to your emotions. Keep a journal. How often are you outraged? Insulted? Angry? Embarrassed? Proud? Fearful? Guilty? Shamed" In his book *Power vs Force* David Hawkins demonstrates that when these emotions are present, we are weak.

If your journaling reveals that you are experiencing these depleting emotions, then move to the energy of the heart, which is courage. Try the heart meditation at the end of this book at least once a day for forty days. Notice how your ability to speak the truth in love improves.

Exercise 5-17: When did you last speak the truth in love? What happened?

5-18: Everyone Wins

Early one morning I listened to a voice mail message from a state officer of an organization I belong to. In the message, she invited herself to our next local meeting and offered to do a presentation that I had already spent several hours preparing and had ready.

My ego exploded. "Who does she think she is? This is intrusion. If I need her help, I'll ask for it!"

Before returning the call, I vowed not to obsess over the matter, but to go to one of my support group meetings, eat breakfast, and meditate.

When I was sure I could speak from my heart and be respectful both to myself and to the other person, I returned the call. I simply explained my effort to prepare and stated I would like to do the program, which I had tailored to our local needs. Through the conversation, we determined that she and her colleague would attend the meeting and be available to augment my remarks and answer questions.

The next day she called back to cancel the visit. In the meantime, her friend had discovered she had to work, and the caller said she was leaving on a trip the day after the meeting and really needed the time to prepare. Via email, she sent me information I didn't have and will add to the presentation. Simple solution.

When I speak from my heart and say what's true for me, everyone wins.

Exercise 5-18: When have you experienced a potentially resentment-producing situation that turned out well?

5-19: Revealing Negative Thinking

For many years I have followed the work of Lynne McTaggert, journalist and author who scientifically proves that change happens when a group focuses on a single intention. In my first class with Lynne McTaggert on "The Power of Intention," her assignment was for me to keep a journal of my negative thinking. I consider myself a positive person, so I thought, "There won't be much in my journal."

Was I ever wrong! I was surprised at the number of times during the day I'm thinking of someone in a critical way—or I focus on something I don't like—or I condemn myself!

This assignment had value for me in two ways. First, I am even more aware that I lose energy when I'm negative. Secondly, the exercise is working much like a fourth step in a 12-step program ("Made a searching and fearless moral inventory of ourselves") in revealing my character flaws. Once they are exposed, then I know what to do. But as long as they remain hidden, I'm weakened.

Exercise 5-19: Write or draw a journal of your negative thinking for a few days. What did you learn about yourself?

5-20: Loving

Love is patient. Love is kind. Love keeps no record of wrongs. *(1 Corinthians 3:4)* This is the checklist I use when I feel ill at ease and know I need to examine my own reactions to people and events. I know I'm happiest and strongest when I'm acting from love. When I'm feeling impatient, unkind, and resentful, I know I'm not in love.

That's when I stop, pivot by remembering what I'm grateful for, and then recite to myself, "Love is patient. Love is kind. Love keeps no record of wrongs."

Exercise 5-20: What do you do to remain loving?

5-21: A Memorable Person

Once I was called in to work with a department that was rife with dissension. The first thing I did was interview each employee privately, seeking to understand how each one fit into the dynamic.

One man I interviewed told this story: He grew up in Africa. When he was very young, both of his parents died, and his country had no plan for caring for orphans. He was on his own. But before he died, his father told him, "Go to school. Get an education." Feeding and clothing himself from trash, he obeyed his father, never missing a day of school. He said, "I paid close attention when I saw parents with their children. I listened to what the parent said, and then I took the words for myself." In this way he learned how to behave.

He came to the attention of the authorities when he was about to graduate at the head of his class. Then the government made sure he had a new suit of clothes and a scholarship to a prestigious university in England. Eventually he came to the U.S., and when I met him, he had a wife, children, and a good job.

Remembering this story always brings me back to the resilience of the human spirit, the power of education, and the utter triviality of most things that trouble us.

Exercise 5-12: Who is a memorable person in your life? What did they teach you?

5-22: Speak the Truth in Love

My nephew died of a heroin overdose. At his memorial service, several young men who had been in treatment with him, spoke. Their stories about my nephew and their shared experiences revealed deep, trusting relationships that came from speaking the truth in love to each other. This truth-telling had transcended other differences, and young men who might not have even liked each other—or ever met in the "real world"—became forever friends. Among other things, that's what people in treatment for addiction learn—how to tell the truth about experiences they would rather forget so that together they can walk through the pain, find healing, and come out more whole.

Ultimately, my nephew lost his life. But he had a few years of sobriety and the experience of loving, trusting relationships.

Exercise 5-22: I find healing from speaking the truth in love. Where do you find it?

5-23: Truth Sets Us Free

The Tulsa Massacre happened in 1921. Although I grew up in Oklahoma, I was unaware of this carnage of African American citizens and businesses that wiped out an entire thriving community. Upon learning about it, my first response was horror and revulsion.

This morning I read about the largest slave auction in the U.S., held in Georgia in 1859—an auction in which 429 men, women, and children were sold. Each of their names was listed.

I'm moving through a range of emotions. I've passed through shame and denial that kept me trapped in unknowing, and now I'm willing to see the whole truth. This is a necessary part of healing. Our nation simply has to do this.

Exercise 5-23: What freedom have you experienced from facing the truth?

5-24: A Parable

A passage from *The Gospel of Mary Magdalene* by Jean-Yves Leloup, p. 69:

A woman was looking for her lost jewels in the village square. The other villagers wished her well and were trying to help her find this treasure in the area in and around the square. They had been searching fruitlessly for some time, when someone asked her: "But exactly where did you lose this treasure?"

"I lost it in my home," the woman answered.

"But are you crazy? If you lost it in your home, why are you having us help you search out here in the square?"

"And you, my friend," she replied, "is this not what you are always doing, searching for your treasure in the streets, in the square, when it is really in your own home that you lost what you most want? Don't you go everywhere in vain search of peace and happiness, your greatest treasure, which you have lost in your own home? In your own heart—that is where you must search. It is there that your treasure has always been waiting to be found."

Exercise 5-24: Where is your treasure? What are you doing to find it? Or how did you find it?

5-25: Light Touch for Heavy Lifting

The filing cabinet in the garage held an accumulation of 20+ years of bank statements, income tax forms, and business information. Some, but not all, of it needed to be shredded. Because the task seemed tedious and monumental, I decided it didn't matter when I finished. I would just do a bit when I wanted.

Here's what astonished me—within a week, it was done. Not only were the files sorted, but also the filing cabinet itself was sold. Unbelievably easy.

If I had told myself, "This has to be done within the week," it would have seemed impossible. I would have resisted, made it hard. As it was, I did heavy lifting with a light touch.

Exercise 5-25: Have you experienced what seems a contradiction? What was it?

5-26: Clarity

Out of all the chaos, confusion, and concern of 2020, I'm grateful for the clarity that has come. I want

- To be informed, not inflamed.
- Food that nourishes, rather than entertains.
- Spiritual practice that feeds my soul.
- Fewer words, more meaning.
- Substance, not sensation.

Exercise 5-26: In 2020, what became clear for you?

Chapter 6 - Reconciliation

Imagine that a storm has just subsided, and you look up to see dissipating black clouds fading into the sun's reflection on lighter clouds, with blue sky as the backdrop.

6-1: Emergence

My father was a meticulous gardener, and he trained me to keep a weed-free landscape with splashes of color, well-trimmed plants, and perfectly mowed grass.

The yard of our new home might be described as desert-rough. Mesquite, yucca, and other native plants some might call weeds prevail. In fact, our gardener tells me that the name for one of them is "snake weed."

Our plan is to live here awhile, observe, and get a better feel for what we want before making major changes. In the process, we've discovered that this yard is a haven for birds—especially gambrel quail—bunnies, and other wildlife. It's delightful—better than watching television. Whatever we do, we want to preserve the native habitat.

We walk in the yard every day, continuing to get a feel for its possibilities, learning to love what is while we imagine what's even better.

Exercise 6-1: What's emerging in your life? How patient are you with the process?

6-2: Facing Challenge

A woman lost her husband many years ago to an unusual accident when he was in his 50's. At the time, she had breast cancer.

Over the next few years, she trekked the Himalayas (something she and her husband had talked about doing), drove in a camper through the western U.S., and ended up in Sedona, where she thought she would die soon.

Every day, she hiked around Bell Rock. Instead of dying, she lived. Then she opened a medical practice for the second time in her life and practiced medicine for another fifteen years.

Now in her 70's, what is noticeable about this woman is her smile. Today when I saw her, she was undeniably radiant.

Exercise 6-2: What challenges are facing you? What might you do?

6-3: What Do You Do?

My friend had just told me the story of her husband's affair with one of her good friends. My question to her was, "How did you forgive him?"

A devout Catholic, she answered, "I went to the chapel, heartbroken. I asked God to remove my hurt and resentment and make it possible for me to forgive them." When at long last she arose to walk out of the church, she was free.

She is still married to her husband and maintains a friendship with her unfaithful friend.

As I think of the emotional storm my friend and her marriage survived, I am reminded of another story about Judge Harold Medina, who presided over the communist trials during the McCarthy era. One day the courtroom erupted and several angry defendants charged the bench.

"In all that excitement, I felt just as calm as I do now when I speak to you; I did not raise my voice over the tone which you hear me use now ...I tell you ...that my unguided will alone and such self-control as I possess were unequal to this test. If ever a man felt the presence of Someone beside him, strengthening his will and giving him aid and comfort, it was I on that day." (*Handbook for Judges,* American Judicature Society, 1961, p.185)

Exercise 6-3 When something in your life erupts and threatens what you hold dear, how would you like to be?

6-4: The Power of Love

She was beautiful and accomplished; he was handsome, funny, and successful. Together they had a beautiful family.

Imagine her shock when he told her he was in love with another woman and wanted a divorce. She felt, in her words, as if "someone had shaken the jar that was my life and then placed it upside down."

Pushing beyond her anger, disappointment, self-righteousness, and hurt, she decided, "I love our family, and I want to keep my marriage."

The decision began a process of healing for both of them. It took time. Today, although their lives aren't perfect, together they have a beautiful family and enjoy their lives.

"Someday, after we have mastered the winds, the waves, and gravity, mankind will harness for God the energy of love. Then, for the second time in the history of the world, we will have discovered fire." Teilhard de Chardin

Exercise 6-4: What in your life needs love? What do you need to push beyond? What are you willing to do?

6-5: The Gift of Forgiveness

A week ago, I cut my finger while cooking. It was a minor cut, but my finger bled so much that I went to Urgent Care to stop the bleeding. Today I have only a minor abrasion to show for the mishap. The swelling and bandages are gone. So it is with physical wounds. Most heal quickly.

Emotional wounds are different. They often throb for years because they are not treated. Instead of crying the tears and seeking help to forgive, we pretend we're not hurt, until the next time, when we pile the new wound on top of the last one. Then we wonder why we aren't happier.

Give yourself the gift of cleansing. Start writing or drawing. Put onto paper everything you haven't forgiven. Then let it go. Forgiveness is a gift for you.

Exercise 6-5: Who do you now forgive?

6-6: Feel the Feelings

An ideal state is to be present—not numbing ourselves with drink or other distraction, but simply being present, feeling our feelings, even the unpleasant ones.

A learned man once taught me that when we tell ourselves, "I don't want to feel sad," (or mad or whatever) our brains hear, "I don't want to feel," and shut down all feelings. We don't feel sad, but we also lose happiness and other good feelings we want. Thus, many people live from task to task, shutting out feeling.

For just a moment today, stop to feel your feelings. Give yourself permission to cry or stomp your feet or shake your fist. Then make a list of what you're grateful for. Do it every day for forty days.

Exercise 6-6: What are you grateful for?

6-7: Forgiveness

Something happened that created the need for me to practice forgiveness. I felt myself feeling like a victim, and I wanted to react like a victim—bitterly and vindictively. But experience has taught me a better way.

To move out of my bitterness, I pulled out a sheet on forgiveness that has floated me through some difficult times. Here are some excerpts:

- Forgiveness is not the approval of the wrong-doing. It is reclaiming my freedom of choice. I choose not to be stuck to another person's actions.

- Forgiveness is a statement that says, "You have no more power over me." I have the courage to let go, turn the page, and start over.

- I don't hate you. I don't fear you. I am free.

May these words be as healing for you as they are for me.

Exercise 6-7: What is forgiveness for you? What do you do when you need to forgive?

6-8: A Way Out of Difficulty

Years ago, my marriage was in difficulty. I was advised to pray, "God, be with him" for Harlan. I did it over and over, numerous times a day, every time I thought of him. Within a very short time, harmony was restored.

When I encounter difficult people today, I pray that same prayer. Sometimes I say it as "Surround and infuse her with love."

The laws of spirituality, neuroscience, and physics align in the power of this prayer.

Exercise 6-8: When you have difficulty with someone, what do you do?

6-9: When a Tempest Arises

Eventually we sailed into a quiet harbor, ate a nourishing breakfast, and then jettied into a quaint little Greek island town. It was a beautiful, clear Sunday, and people were wading on the beach or having coffee outdoors or, like us, simply walking along the shore.

Beyond the harbor, the ocean's mighty waves still churned. But we were safe, serene, relaxed, and happy.

Exercise 6-9: When a tempest arises, what do you do to maintain equanimity?

6-10: Dealing with Disappointment

The day before our first dinner party in our new home, the utility room flooded and spilled over onto the kitchen floor. Even more significant than the physical exertion of mopping up the water was the anxiety that overcame me in the twenty-four hours we waited for the plumber to arrive. How serious is the problem? Will we have to un-invite our guests? If so, what will I do with all this food?

I want to live in gratitude—peace—calm. I know that stress is my choice; I don't have to go there on the whim of circumstance. But disappointment seems to be my default setting when things don't go according to my plan.

What ultimately happened is that the plumber fixed the problem with plenty of time left for dinner preparation. All my stress and worry were wasted negative energy.

Today I intend to change my emotional default so that I remain calm and trusting, no matter what.

Exercise 6-10: What's your default when things don't go according to your plan? What would you like it to be?

6-11: January

> January, a gray month.
> Allergy season.
> Cold.
> Through the muck of it all,
> Shine the light of love into my heart.
> Lift the clouds.
> Let the sun shine through.

Exercise 6-11: I wondered if the word "muck" were right for this piece. Then I learned that one definition for "muck" is "fertilizer." Perfect. What is the month of January fertilizing for you?

6-12: Bunnies and Coyotes

Each morning as I stand in front of my bathroom mirror, I'm also watching the bunnies grazing in the yard outside—two larger rabbits and two smaller. Somehow it brings me peace to watch them eating breakfast just before I eat mine.

The last few nights we've heard coyotes howling, marauding through our neighborhood, while I, in my warm, safe bed, hope the bunnies cling tightly to the inner bushes and go unnoticed.

Today when I looked out the window, I saw one bunny. Harlan says the others are in the bushes, being cautious, but I fear he's wrong, trying to mend my broken heart.

I'm letting my heart be broken, and I long for a world without coyotes.

Exercise 6-12: What do you long for? What do you do when your heart is broken?

6-13: Return Home

On the first day of my return home, I sit in bed with my coffee and look out the window to the wispy soft white cloud in the distance, lying peacefully among the trees. Beyond, I see the red roofs and tall Italian cypress of our village, snuggled into the base of the foothills of the Mogollon Rim.

I feel the shackles around my heart and soul fall away as I put the memory of metal and concrete, traffic, and hard edges, from my visit to the city, behind me.

My surroundings feed or starve my soul. I choose nature's welcome. Home.

Exercise 6-13: What is home to you?

6-14: Holy Place

I headed to my favorite hiking trail, my place of solace and refuge.

I stopped in my favorite place—my cathedral—a plateau with a 360-degree view. To my left was Cathedral Rock. As I slowly turned left, there was Bell Rock, then Courthouse Butte, Gibraltar, and right in front of me, Baby Bell. In the distance was the chapel, hidden by the trees and hills, and then Thunder Mountain with Coxcomb in the distance. I breathed deeply, gave thanks, finished my hike, and then rested.

I followed the trailhead to the parking lot, got into my car, and eased it into the living traffic.

Exercise 6-14: What is your holy place?

6-15: Two-a-Day

One of the truths that became clear to me when I began my spiritual journey is that what I focus on, gets stronger.

When I found myself distraught over one bad news report after another, I decided that, instead of attending to current events, I would focus on performing two actions every day that make my part of the world a better place.

In the morning, I think about what those two actions will be. They don't have to be large or earth-shaking. As I perform them, I am aware of good energy. At the end of the day, I give thanks.

Will you join me?

Exercise 6-15: What two actions might you take to make your part of the world better?

6-16: Miracle with a Sense of Humor

My dear friend Lindy Segall shared this story with me:

Thanks to flight delay, I found myself trudging through La Guardia Airport at rush hour (an oxymoron in the city that never sleeps). Taxis hopelessly gridlocked. Made a snap decision to try the MTA, something I'd never done before. Stopped at Eddie Bauer shop to ask for directions.

A shy young salesperson started to point the way, then changed her mind. She walked me to the station, advised me on metro card purchase, and then guided me to the turnstile, making sure I was on the correct path to the E train. I shook her hand and thanked her.

"I'm Lindy. What's your name?"

She replied with a sweet smile. "Divinity."

Exercise 6-16: Do you have an example of a miracle with a sense of humor? Or an experience with being lost?

6-17: Thread the Needle

A phrase in the third step prayer from the *Big Book of Alcoholics Anonymous* goes, "Relieve me of the bondage of self," to be neither more than nor less than who we truly are. Ego is tricky. Sometimes it inflates us into believing we are entitled to get what we want; other times, it convinces us we are not worthy of receiving good. Joy in life comes from "threading the needle," and the eye of the needle is the heart.

Exercise 6-17: When have you felt fulfilled, as if you were in exactly the right place, doing exactly the right thing? Where in your body do you feel it?

6-18: Breathe in Love

Often, with a choice between being in stress and being in love, I rock a bit between the two. A solution that works is to spend forty-five minutes in meditation, breathing in love and breathing out everything else. It helps. It brings peace. If you don't have forty-five minutes, try ten.

Exercise 6-18: What might you do when you have a choice between stress and ease?

6-19: From Splintered to Whole

A young friend described her life. Two toddlers, one of whom is potty training. A thriving career. A marriage. Leadership in a nonprofit that she's devoted to. Her home the market with a move imminent. She finds herself crying, with a feeling of being out of control.

As I listened to her story, the image that came to me was "splintered." In each of these roles, only a piece of her is showing up—the piece with the expertise to handle that thing. She seemed to be losing her sense of wholeness, even though she was so grateful for all the goodness in her life. After the whole story was out, I asked, "Would you like to write an intention?"

Here's what we wrote: In the midst of seeming chaos, I breathe and realize I am alive. I am whole. I am present.

Exercise 6-19: Do you ever feel splintered? What might you do differently to feel whole?

6-20: Still Learning

Still I am learning that my life is one whole, not a string of boxes with different rules. What governs my spiritual life—love, compassion, forgiveness, grace—is powerful in every aspect of living. Let the walls come down.

Exercise 6-20: What are you still learning? What do you wish?

6-21: The Power of Holding One's Peace

As a participant in an angry exchange, I met anger with anger. Although I ultimately accepted the other person's apology, my system was still full of the chemistry of anger that took days to let go.

Yesterday, as an observer, I witnessed the power of holding one's peace when anger erupts. One person attacked. The other person remained calm, reaffirmed his love, and exuded peace. The effect on the angry person was that he quickly calmed. It's possible. It's powerful.

Exercise 6-21: What is your response when anger comes at you?

6-22: Two Stories of Forgiveness

A *60 Minutes* episode (May 12th 2019) featured two women who had experienced the power of forgiveness. One had lost her brother because of a drunk driver. The other had been injured for life by a gunman. Both of these women suffered from their own anger and outrage over what had happened to them, so they ultimately sought the help of a program called Restorative Justice. Mediators brought them face to face with the imprisoned perpetrators.

Through the Restorative Justice process, they gave their forgiveness and reaffirmed the worth and value of the other person. Healing occurred, all around.

Another example of forgiveness that comes to mind is the Amish parents whose children were killed in their school in 2006. That very evening these parents went to the gunman's home to express their sympathy and forgiveness to his wife and children, who had also experienced a loss that day.

Exercise 6-22: What's your experience with forgiveness? Is there someone you need to forgive?

6-23: More on Forgiveness

- Forgiveness occurs when you systematically lay aside conclusions you have reached about other people and the motivations for their actions. (Maria Nemeth, *The Energy of Money,* 1997)

- Forgiveness is not the approval of the wrongdoing. It is reclaiming my freedom of choice.

- Forgiveness is not weakness. It is strength of character. I have the courage to let go, turn the page, and start over. It is a statement that says, "You have no more power over me."

- To forgive does not mean that I need to like you or approve of what you do. It means I understand your dis-ease. It means I don't hate you. I don't fear you. I am free. You can't hurt me anymore. I have the wisdom and strength to make choices.

- Resentments and anger are self-punishment. Forgiveness is self-nurturing.

- The Spanish derivation for "resent" is "resentir," which literally means "to feel again."

Thus, when we choose not to forgive, we choose to feel the original hurt again—and again—and again.

Exercise 6-23: What is your experience with forgiveness?

6-24: Help

Here is a favorite page from *The Boy, the Mole, the Fox, and the Horse* by Charles Mackesy:

"What is the bravest thing you've ever said?" asked the boy.

"Help," said the horse.

This page hits home because I spent so many years believing that asking for help was a sign of weakness—that I needed to do everything independently and perfectly, finding all the answers within myself. Finally, I hit a challenge that I simply could not live through on my own. I asked for help. Then it got easier to ask for help.

Just yesterday I misplaced a gift certificate that had been donated for our church's auction to alleviate hunger. I had a system. Two pieces of paper had fallen through my system and were nowhere to be found. I looked and looked. Then I asked for help. Before the day ended, helpers had come, and now, in less than 24 hours, I have everything I need.

Do my helpers think less of me for having to ask for their help? No. In fact, asking others for help strengthens relationships.

Exercise 6-24: What is your experience with asking for help?

Chapter 7 - Love is Quiet

When she was about three years old, I took my oldest granddaughter to Portland, OR, to visit her aunt, my daughter. We went to an aquarium and paused for a long time to watch, through glass, two sea lions underwater. Imagine turquoise waters and an overhanging rock shelf, protecting the couple. What struck me was how quiet it must be to them, underwater.

7-1: Friendship

Flowing through life is a
Stream called friendship.
For years, I played on its banks,
Pretending I didn't need the water.
Then calamity fell, and I poured
Out my heart to the person who was there,
My friend.
She accepted my darkness,
Blessed it, banished it.
It was then that I waded into the water,
Splashed in its healing.
Since, friends have been many,
Each unique, yet the same.
The universal heart flows through all of us.

When we move into it, we are one.

Exercise 7-1: What is your experience with friendship?

7-2: Companion

As he handed me the plastic Southwest Airlines pass, he asked, "Will you be my companion?" Then I began my long journey to learn how to be a worthy companion.

My mother's advice to me had been, "Get a good education. Never have to depend on a man." From her perspective, it was good advice. Her experience was to accept unacceptable behavior because she didn't believe she could make it on her own.

I, on the other hand, know how to make it on my own. I choose to be married, and I'm still learning how to be a good companion without losing myself.

Most of what I've learned is wordless. My marriage flows, and I flow with it. It's not about getting my way or who wins. It's all about seeking the greater good, which, as it turns out, is good for both of us.

Exercise 7-2: What is your vision of companionship?

7-3: Transition

Today our first granddaughter left for college. How can that be?

I saw her take her first breath—heard her first cry—watched her through the joys and pains of childhood and confusion of adolescence.

Today she opens a door to a bigger world of possibility.

Grant her confidence, peace, assurance, and success in a happy college life.

Exercise 7-3: What is your prayer today for someone in transition?

7-4: A Thanksgiving Prayer

After a long drive with excited children, we would pull into my mother's driveway. Immediately, I felt relief. For the next few days of Thanksgiving, I relaxed in safety and plenty. I was home.

Mother left that home many years ago. She no longer creates perfect Thanksgivings except in memory. I still miss the feeling of total relaxation when I walked through her door and total delight when I opened her refrigerator.

This year our children will walk through our door to celebrate Thanksgiving. May they have total relaxation and peace in being here.

In gratitude, infuse our home, our food, our hearts, with love that heals and replenishes. The love I learned from my mother.

Exercise 7-4: What is a treasured memory of your mother? Or what was your most special Thanksgiving?

7-5: Snow

Outside my window, light, wet snow is falling. The horizon is shrouded, a blur of whiteness. Accented against the dark trees, the snow gently falls as I sit, transfixed.

The gentle snow is relaxing, calming, restorative. It freshens and lifts my spirit. It says, "Everything that is past is over. I'm refreshing your life."

Exercise 7-5: In the winter season, what refreshes and renews you?

7-6: Where Is Love?

Sometimes I get so distracted by what's going on around me that I fail to notice the love that's right in front of me. One morning, as Harlan and I walked out of our hotel in

Las Vegas, I was silently annoyed by the loud music and frenetic jangling of all the games.

As we opened the door to go out, I noticed a homeless woman on the street cradling something in her arms. I was focused on my destination, but I did see she was holding and petting a dog. We walked past her. Then Harlan stopped and said, "I'm going to give her some money."

As I waited for him, I realized I was in the presence of love, in the form of a homeless person and her pet. Sometimes love shows up in unexpected places.

Exercise 7-6: When has love unexpectedly showed up for you?

7-7: Just One Day

> Just one day of
> Lighter eating,
> And my weight drops.
> Just one day of
> Exercises, and my
> Knee hurts less.
> Just one day in
> Meditation, and my
> Heart has peace.

Exercise 7-7: What is the power of one day that you have experienced?

7-8: Sacred Home

> So much of my life
> Is routine.
> Brush teeth—groom
> Myself—dress.
> Pick up papers—

Tidy the room.
Take out trash—
Feed the dogs—
Water the plants—
Walk.
With lightness and gratitude,
I do it all in peace.
Sacred home.

Exercise 7-8: What is sacred home to you?

7-9: Hospitality Revised

I just said goodbye to my cousin and her friends, who are now my friends, and I am a bit sad, but mostly grateful. Grateful that she came and grateful that my view of hospitality has changed.

When I was young, I believed that hospitality was making everything perfect. I was misguided and, by the time my guests left, I was exhausted. I'm sure they felt my depleted energy.

Today I simply want my guests to relax and have a good time. This means cooking simple recipes in advance, ready to warm. It means getting out of the house and enjoying the area with them. It means being relaxed myself.

Our home is simple, peaceful, and easy. That's how I want guests to feel. If something is imperfect, I don't care.

Exercise 7-9: When do you feel most welcome? How do you do hospitality?

7-10: My Soul Expands

Our land stops at the rail fence,
Yet I can see beyond.
My eyes follow the slope of the hill down
To the pond and the tops of trees growing

From the valley below.
Then my eyes rise to the rooftops and
Italian cypress in the village,
Lifting to the bluish gray hills beyond.
My soul expands.

Exercise 7-10: When do you feel your soul expand?

7-11: Impatience and Deliverance

Leaky plumbing and a three-day wait for a fix. A misdiagnosis that turned out, ten days later, to be allergy to cedar.

Out of the totality of my life, these two mere occurrences fed the monster of impatience so that it filled all but a bit of space in my life. I was trapped, with no room to breathe.

Then a phone call came from a friend—then one from another friend—then my daughter—then yet another friend. The freedom of love swept impatience away.

Coincidence? I think not.

Exercise 7-11: When has love set you free?

7-12: Love Yourself

When I started recovery from workaholism and relationship difficulties, one of my teachers suggested that every day I write a love letter to myself—not one that would feed my ego, but one that would nurture my heart.

I wrote simply, "Nancy, I love that you're taking time to sit and be warmed in the sun." Or "I love how calm you were through the computer problems. Well done."

Simply and easily, I was building self-esteem and capacity for love.

Over the years, I have recommended this practice to others. Few do it. Do you have the courage to write a love letter to yourself?

Exercise 7-12: What do you love about yourself? What are you doing to increase your capacity for love?

7-13: Grace and Mercy

Last Sunday, Harlan and I served as ushers for our small church. One of the duties is to light the altar candles at the beginning of the service and extinguish them at the end.

Later that evening, as I lay in bed awaiting sleep, I sat up with a jolt, realizing I had not extinguished the candles. Panic overcame me as I visualized the church in flames, and I felt a strong urge to drive there—alone—in the dark—through rain and lightning.

Then I took some deep breaths, started journaling, and asked God to do for me what I could not do. As my mind calmed, I considered possibilities. The candles are on tall brass candlesticks on a stone altar—not likely to ignite anything. Then I realized that whoever cleared the communion paraphernalia from the altar would have seen the candles still burning and extinguished them.

I gave thanks to be part of a church were people see what needs to be done and simply do it, regardless of whose responsibility it is. Grace. Mercy.

I slept peacefully and drove to the church first thing the next morning. The candles were not lit. No one ever mentioned to me my oversight.

Exercise 7-13: When has someone given you grace and mercy?

7-14: Under a Rainbow

I fell asleep under a rainbow.

After the rain and darkness,
The setting sun broke through the clouds,
Showering the hills with soft light.
Above the hills, on the dark gray clouds,
A rainbow appeared, stayed, floated against the clouds.
I fell asleep under that rainbow
And awakened with the dark of a new day.

Exercise 7-14: Author and Franciscan Priest Richard Rohr says, "The entire visible universe is manifestation of God." When have you experienced this truth?

7-15: A Quiet Thing

A friend remarked, "I wish I could recapture the bright light of feeling that something wonderful is about to happen!"

Something wonderful has happened. She has a good marriage. A great career. Happy, healthy children. Many friends and meaningful relationships.

I said to her, "You have matured. That bright, shiny feeling of something new may have faded. But it's not gone. You're living in the glow. Things don't 'knock you off your feet' like they used to.

Lyrics to a song I love go like this: "When it all comes true, just the way you planned, it's funny but the bells don't ring. It's a quiet thing. When you hold the world in your trembling hand, you think you'd hear a choir sing. But it's a quiet thing. There are no exploding fireworks. Where's the roaring of the crowds? Maybe it's the strange new atmosphere way up here among the clouds. But I don't hear the drums and I don't hear the band—the sounds I'm told such moments bring. Happiness comes in on tiptoe. It's a quiet thing. A quiet thing. A very quiet thing."

Exercise 7-15: Today, how do you respond to wonderful experiences?

7-16: A Miracle

I went to a shop in tourist-laden Uptown Sedona because I love the owners, even though I could have purchased the item I was after in a store with more accessible parking.

As I walked from the far end of the parking lot, an older couple, looking lost, caught my eye. The man asked, "Where is the tourist office where we can get maps?"

I said, "Walk with me. I'll show you."

They were from San Francisco, and it was their only day in Sedona, so I became a walking tour guide, advising them on must-sees. Then the tourist office was in sight, so I said good-bye and wished them well.

My shopping completed, I headed back to my car to drive home. As my car approached the tourist office, there they were—she, sitting on a bench; he, taking photographs. I pulled up to the curb. "I'll take you back to your car." It was a long walk, and she moved with a cane.

I left them at their car, ready to find the Chapel of the Holy Cross, with its spectacular view. What I know without a doubt is that I received more joy than I gave.

Exercise 7-16: When have you given kindness? When have you received it?

7-17: Go to Neutral

When other people say or do what you don't want or like, set your emotional state on neutral. Don't try to change them. Accept that you can't explain sight to a blind person.

After you have relaxed into your neutral state, move to compassion, a manifestation of love. Quiet, loving presence is a powerful force.

Exercise 7-17: When was the last time you were with someone you wanted to change? What did you do? How well did it work?

7-18: The Energy of Things

An interior designer advised me to surround myself with what I loved and get rid of everything else. I discarded everything I had bought because it was trendy or because someone said I should have it. What was left was what I loved.

In my next cleaning, I picked up the elephants that were the mascot for our marriage. The "Hallelujah Lady" who is the theme for my life. The Ansel Adams photographs my daughter gave me. The art from very special artists. I could go on.

It has taken awhile for me to learn what I love. Through the years, I have discarded much. Today I am surrounded by what I love.

Exercise 7-18: What are you surrounded by? What energy does it give?

7-19 No Words

Some news yesterday left me speechless. Something within me said I should have something wise or clever to say, but I don't. Some experiences simply go beyond words. So, for now, I remain silent.

Exercise 7-19: When was the last time you had no words?

7-20: Love Is a Decision

Love is patient. Love is kind. Love keeps no record of wrongs. I strive to live within the circle of Love.

But last week, on two consecutive days, I had challenges. People were not giving me what I thought I deserved. The first time it happened, I forced the issue and got what I wanted, with a few ruffled feathers from those whom I accosted. I didn't call anyone any names, but my forceful energy was clear, and I felt that I needed to make amends, which I did.

The second time it happened, on the very next day, I remembered how bad I had felt the day before while accosting others. Thus, I made a decision to accept what is and be gracious. Before I left that office, everyone was thanking me for my patience. Love is a decision.

Exercise 7-20: When have you made a decision to stay in love instead of venting your frustration?

7-21: Valentine's Day

It took me many, many years to learn how to love. I still do it imperfectly. Here is my experience of love as I understand it today.

Love...

- Accepts what is.
- Shares the last bite.
- Acknowledges presence.
- Gives grace.
- Says, "I'll do that for you."
- Is quiet.

Exercise 76-21: What is your understanding of love today?

7-22: Almost Every Hour

Richard Rohr is one of my most treasured teachers. This morning I read through some notes I took from a talk he gave in 2017. I wrote, "To be loving has to be chosen almost every hour."

I realized anew that my efforts to be loving once and for all are futile. It's good to be reminded that to be loving is a continual decision.

Exercise 7-22: What is your experience with continually choosing to love?

7-23: Power of a Safe Presence

Two young girls came into an unfamiliar group of mostly older adults. At first, they were hesitant and reserved. Then, so gradually, they began to interact with the people around them. Then I saw smiles as they relaxed into the acceptance and grace they experienced.

As I observed this transformation, I committed anew to being a safe presence for others.

Exercise: 7-23 How do make a safe presence for others? How do you create safe space for yourself?

7-24: Friendship

Between my friend and me is an invisible stream. We float.

Exercise 7-24: How does friendship seem to you?

7-25: What We See Is What We're Looking With

"There's nothing either good or bad but thinking makes it so." *Hamlet*

"What we see is not what we're looking at, but what we're looking with, so let us find our eyes of love." *Twelve-step Saying*

When I read the first quotation above, I was still in school. I thought, "That's right." When I heard the second quotation, I was in the early stages of Al-Anon recovery, and I understood it meant for me to take action. Knowing something intellectually is not sufficient without the action step.

I have more work to do in finding my eyes of love. How about you?

Exercise 7-25: Whose behavior is giving you a problem? When you look at that person through eyes of love, how important is it?

7-26: Love Completely

In honor of my recently deceased 37-year-old nephew, Austin, yesterday I watched the movie *A River Runs Through It*. I chose that movie because Austin loved fly fishing, and I wanted to feel the oneness with nature that he felt on the river.

Near the end of the movie was a line that reached into my heart and resonated as true. "We can love completely, without complete understanding."

Exercise 7-26: What is your understanding of love?

7-27: Unlearning

As I've aged, I realize that what I once accepted as "iron-clad rules" might not be so. A house, for example, does not need thorough cleaning every week. A tiny spider web might mean that a tiny spider has been busy for the last few minutes; it's not a symbol of filth.

In a different realm, I've learned that I don't have to respond to everything I disagree with or don't like. I can choose to be silent.

Our visiting minister said, without being specific, that in retirement he is unlearning previously held beliefs.

Exercise 7-27: What are you unlearning? What would you like to unlearn?

7-28: What to Do with Feelings

Through recovery, I've been learning what to do with feelings. For several years I've taken the slogan, "How important is it?" to mean that my feelings are unimportant, irrelevant. Brush them away and move on. But now I know that feelings cannot be repressed without repercussions. Eventually, they WILL be expressed!

I've also learned that all feelings are right and good.

Having accepted my feelings, I am free to decide what expression will contribute to my well-being and that of others. That is the challenge.

In my meditation this morning, these words came, "Let all that you do be done in love." (I Corinthians 16:14)

Love for ourselves and others is the screen to pass our feelings through.

Exercise 7-28: What do you do with feelings? Are you happy with your choice?

7-29: The Power of Love

Each of us is a vibrational field, surrounded by other vibrational fields. What we feel affects these fields. We sense when others are uneasy—when they are truthful—when they are loving. Others sense us, as well. Truth and love have more power than falsity. (For more information, read David Hawkins' book, *Power vs Force*.)

The challenge is to be true and to love, even in the face of lies and hatred.

Exercise 7-30: When have you been changed by the power of love coming from someone else?

7-31: Dutch Babies

One of our favorite breakfast dishes is Dutch babies, flat pancakes served with toasted almonds, berries, and a heap of powdered sugar on top. I add a couple of slices of bacon on the side.

During the pandemic, we invited friends, one couple at a time, for breakfast on our back patio, which has a splendid view of the red rocks of Sedona.

Most of the time, our friends have stayed all morning, visiting and enjoying the conversation and fresh air. We treasure these simple times. We want to keep this practice when we no longer "have to."

Exercise 7-31: What pandemic practice do you want to keep? What were some good things that came out of it?

7-32: Gift for the Heart

My brother is a late sleeper. When I visited him in his new home, a seven-hour drive from Sedona, we had a wonderful time. Days later, when I was ready to return home, I planned to leave early in the morning. The night before, I said, "Don't bother to get up. I can let myself out."

The next morning when I arose, I saw him through the patio doors, sitting outside in the dark. That sight touched my heart. In spite of his aversion to morning, he was there for me.

Exercise 7-32: When has someone given your heart a gift?

Chapter 8 - Be Still

Imagine a great blue heron standing oh, so still, blending into the tall grass at the edge of a pond, almost invisible.

8-1: In Plain Sight

With our neighbors, we share land at the tip of the cul-de-sac. Weeds have grown, browned, become unruly to the extent that we have agreed to do something. Clearly, the offending weedy plants are to be removed.

The question is do we plant something in their place? Something more beautiful? We've thrown around several ideas—lavender, wildflowers, native grasses.

This morning, as I looked over my own back yard, I saw a solution. Gopher weed. It's a succulent with a beautiful yellow bloom in the spring. It's blooming right now. Yesterday I walked among the plants and found no weeds, so that tells me it blocks out weeds. It's easy to grow; in fact, it has to be thinned. We have plenty of excess plants that could be transplanted, watered for a short time until they get established, and then left alone.

It seems a perfect solution that was right in front of me all the time while I stretched to find a way.

Exercise 8-1: When have you struggled with a decision when the solution was in front of you all the time?

8-2: Lull

In between intense periods of frenetic activity, there came a lull.

Lull is the space between two pauses. It's calmer than a pause. Quieter.

In a lull, there's nothing to be done. No one to contact. No list to check. No worry. No thought.

Lull opens the door for rest—nothingness—the quiet joy of being.

Exercise 8-2: Describe your last lull.

8-3: Eyes on the Horizon

As the boat pitched and yawed in the waters of the Aegean, provoked by Meltimi winds, my host said, "Keep your eyes on the horizon to avoid being seasick." From that moment on, as my body bounced and slid, my stomach remained calm because my eyes were fixed on that thin blue line where ocean meets sky.

Eventually, we sailed into a quiet harbor, ate a nourishing breakfast, and then jettied into a quaint little island town

Beyond the harbor, the sea still raged, but we were safe, serene, and happy.

Exercise 8-3: When a tempest arises, what do you do to remain calm?

8-4: Whisper Time

This is a whisper time of my life. The shouted demands of young family and career are silent. The inner, urgent voice for more, faster, sooner is still.

The whisper that is rising is exquisite: Appreciation for a pasta sauce that I made myself—for sunset and sunrise—for simply spending time with someone I love—for the peace of an overcast day.

Exercise 8-4: How would you describe this time of your life?

8-5: Pause

Thanksgiving is put away, and a glimmer of Christmas peeks from my mantle. Splashes of the season to come are unpacked and displayed, and the tree stands ready to be decorated.

But today, what I need most is pause. No season to clean up or prepare for. Just pause.

I don't know how long my pause will last. I only know I'm relishing silence, with both dogs napping and Harlan on the golf course. Nature outside is going its own way.

As for me, I'm on pause.

Exercise: 8-5 Have you recuperated from the last season? Are you regenerated for the next one? If not, when will you pause?

8-6: Silence

> At some stage in the
> Process to find peace,
> Words leave.
> What remains is silence.

Exercise 8-6: What does silence sound like to you? When has peaceful silence come for you?

8-7: An Experience with Meditation

Once a month I participate in a group meditation. We meet in a church, and last week the choir was rehearsing nearby as we started our meditation.

"Breathe deeply through the nose and exhale slowly through the mouth." I focused on my breathing. I just kept breathing.

After awhile choir rehearsal was over. I became aware that conversations were happening—some just outside our door. But I was more aware of my breathing and felt no need to quieten anyone.

I was meditating. The choir was dispersing. We were on parallel tracks.

Exercise 8-7: When have you been aware but not disturbed by something on a parallel track?

8-8: Choose

Sometimes, things happen
That are so far beyond
My understanding—
That all I can do is
Be silent and wait.
Maybe, in my lifetime,
The answer will not come.
In the meantime, I choose
Peace, gratitude, and love.

Exercise 8-8: What do you do when the answer does not come? How do you live with not understanding?

8-9: Flow

A sadness comes over me
When I've done what I dreamed of.
I grieve the loss of a dream,
Even small, inconsequential ones.
I long to live in the flow,
Not the episodes, of life.

Exercise: 8-9 What does living the flow, not the episodes, of life mean to you?

8-10: Ephemeral Life

> I want to seize and hold
> Precious moments in life—
> Say, "Sit. Freeze,"
> So they last.
> But the Law says,
> "Flow."
> So I release my longing
> For permanence.
> In gratitude, I embrace
> Ephemeral Life.

Exercise 8-11: How are you living the days of your life? Are you trying to freeze them or allow them to flow? What does that look like?

8-12: Life Bursting Forth

> Beneath those bushes
> Is life about to burst forth.
> There must be nests
> Because I see adult
> Gambel quail scurrying about,
> Watching protectively from atop the
> Fence, and waiting
> For life to burst forth.

Exercise 8-12: Where around you do you see life about to burst forth?

8-13: Morning Meditation

I sit up straight. I close my eyes. I breathe deeply, slowly, regularly. I place my fingers on a string of beads, moving slowly from bead to bead to help me stay in the moment.

My mind flits into the past, reviewing what has gone before. I re-center, go to the next bead, and focus on my breathing.

My mind leaps forward, anticipating what lies ahead. More quickly this time, I re-center and focus on my breathing. I begin to let the breath breathe me.

I become aware of the warm sunlight on my forehead. From somewhere, deep within, I feel these words: "Be still and know that I am God."

Exercise 8-13: How do you experience meditation?

8-14: From Doing to Being

A young woman came to me for guidance to live a happier, more peaceful life. I taught her some tools for taking responsibility for her own emotional state and shared a few daily practices for maintaining peace and harmony.

About three weeks went by. Then she called to say, "Things are going well, but is there more I should be doing?" She was experiencing discomfort from the switch from doing to being.

My answer to her was, "Just keep it up. There is no more you have to do. Enjoy your life and share your good news with someone you trust."

Exercise 8-14: Do you find yourself looking for more to DO to be fulfilled? Do you share your happiness with someone you trust?

8-15: Faith

As I slept, snow fell. Looking out over my white world the next morning, I see clouds meeting the hills, completely obscuring the familiar Bell Rock and Courthouse Butte from my view. Yet I know, within the clouds, they are still there.

Exercise 8-15: When in your life has your faith been dim? How did you find it again?

8-16: Windshield Wipers

At a spiritual conference, one of the presenters, Cynthia Bourgeault, used this analogy: If during contemplation or meditation, your mind won't stop chattering, imagine a pair of windshield wipers that clear it. If, once your mind is clear, the chatter comes back, imagine that you've set the wipers on "intermittent" and see them clear the space again.

Since I heard this powerful analogy, I've used it not just for meditation, but for all the negative, critical, or discouraging thoughts that sometimes lodge in my mind. Windshield wipers. It works.

Exercise 8-16: What do you do when mental chatter gets in the way of your peace of mind?

8-17: What Brings Me Peace

> Quiet—Sun dappling through green leaves
> Soft rain—Flowers simply blooming

Exercise 8-17: What brings you peace today?

8-18: Peace

> On this soft summer morning

The distant hum of mowers—
Sun sifting through mesquites.
A white dog licks her paws.
I celebrate peace.

Exercise 8-19: What gives you peace?

8-20: Tamales

Some people might call it coincidence; others, synchronicity. I call it answer to prayer, from this definition of prayer I learned as a teenager: "Prayer is the soul's sincerest desire, uttered or unexpressed." These days I keep myself in the place of possibility through daily meditation and consciously choosing love, grace, and peace above all else.

Here's what happened: My daughter and son-in-law will arrive for a visit on the day that Harlan and I return from a trip. We'll meet at the airport. All good, except that I won't have my typical week-before-a-visitor-comes to cook and prepare. I wondered if Virginia might agree to make for us some of her wonderful tamales, realizing that she typically does that at Christmas, and this is August.

Moments later, the phone rang. Virginia. She said, "I'm making tamales this week-end. Would you like some?"

"Thank you, God," I said, realizing that no request is too small.

Exercise 8-20: How does answer to prayer manifest for you?

8-21: Dawdling

Dawdling has always been one of my favorite things to do. I give my mind permission to float me for a while. This morning's dawdling involved battery-run candles. For two or three years, those candles with dead batteries had lain on the bottom of a drawer.

My dawdling mind doesn't put things off. It has nothing else to do! It says, "Let's do that right now!"

To my utter amazement, I found batteries that fit and was able to light the light, which is now glowing from a favorite Frank Lloyd Wright-inspired glass candle holder. To my even greater amazement, the whole task took only a few minutes.

Dawdling brings me pleasure and contentment.

Exercise 8-21: What brings you effortless pleasure and contentment?

8-22: Just Breathe

As I sat to meditate, I immediately became aware of my shallow, rapid breathing. I was late. I parked the car and walked quickly up the stairs, the last one to take my place in the group. I wasn't able to begin the meditation with the group. My first task was to slow my breathing and clear my mind.

That's what we do, isn't it? We're running late, or someone says something we don't like. Our breathing becomes shallow, and our stress rises.

A friend sometimes tells me of her many distresses. I say to her, "Just breathe." When we are focused on breathing, we cannot be focused on that which is beyond our control.

Exercise 8-22: Right now, how are you breathing?

8-23: Wait and See

I stopped feeding the birds because of the hawks who swooped into their midst and inevitably caught one to devour. Today the birds in our yard find their own food—and there's plenty. I simply sit at the window watching, at close range, the bluebirds and house finches feast on the tree's berries.

A friend called, concerned over someone's actions and harsh words. After talking it through, she decided to do nothing—to wait and see what happened. What happened was reconciliation, with no effort at all from my friend.

When we accept what is—stand back—do nothing, we leave space for God to work. Actually, we aren't doing nothing. We're living in faith.

Exercise 8-23: What situation in your life is calling you to stand back and do nothing?

8-24: Thoreau and Medoff

Henry David Thoreau, in *Walden*, wrote, "I went to the woods because I wished to live deliberately, to front only the essential facts of life, and see if I could not learn what it had to teach."

On June 23, 2019, *Sixty Minutes'* Leslie Stahl interviewed Marshall Medoff, an 81-year-old man from Massachusetts with no science background who decided he wanted to find "environmentally friendly transportation fuels in a clean and cost-effective way." To begin his journey, like Thoreau, he went to Walden, immersing himself in nature and solitude. In his words, "What I thought was the reason people were failing [to find fuel solutions] is they were trying to overcome nature instead of working with it." Long story short, more than a decade after he went to Walden, Medoff has built a company and success in accomplishing his dream.

His journey began with communion with nature, peace in silence, openness to perceive, and faith in a favorable outcome.

Exercise 8-24: When have you experienced success that began with silence or meditation or immersing yourself in nature?

8-25: Listen and Wait

Amazing Austin artist Ash Almonte, who created the cover for this book, donated an embellished print of a hummingbird for an auction to benefit food banks in the Verde Valley of Arizona. A Sedona framer agreed to donate the framing, and while it was in his shop, a woman came in, saw the hummingbird, and burst into tears. She explained to the framer that her mother, who had recently died, promised to return to her in the form of a hummingbird. She wanted to buy the piece.

Our auction team agreed we should offer to sell it to her, but she didn't take our offer. We were puzzled, but we put it back into the auction collection and hung it on the wall along with other auction pieces.

The next morning it was discovered that the hummingbird had fallen from its hook, and the glass had shattered, but the art was not damaged. Now I'll take it back to the frame shop to have the glass replaced.

I remarked, "This hummingbird is trying to tell us something. I'm listening, but I don't get it." Then I realized—sometimes I'm just supposed to listen and wait.

Exercise 8-26: When has something puzzling happened to you, and the only thing to do was listen and wait?

8-27: Sacred Powerlessness

A heavy snowfall has made my world white and still. No coffee meetings. No trips to the grocery store or anywhere else. No "what if" or "maybe." Just sacred powerlessness as it snows. Peace.

Exercise 8-27: When have you felt sacred powerlessness?

8-28: Who Do You Want to Learn From?

My 95-year-old friend has a sparkle in her eyes and always a smile. Yesterday another friend asked her, "What is your secret for your long life?" She responded, "I just watch life go by [and I don't let anything upset me.]"

This amazing woman had not been idle. She was a chemist by profession. She was a state leader of a nonprofit to benefit women's education. She is a mother. She helped her son start a business.

The state of mind she was describing was not apathy; it was equanimity. I want to learn all that I can from her.

Exercise 8-28: Who do you want to learn from? What do you want to learn?

8-29: Miracle at Moraine Lake

One August I traveled to Canada with my daughter, Anne Marie, and daughter-in-law Scotti. We saw the Northern Lights in Yellowknife and then made our way to Banff, which included a tour of Lake Louise and finally to Moraine Lake, a turquoise, glacier-fed, quiet body of water.

My daughter hiked to the very top of a tall pile of rocks to view the lake from a higher perspective. My daughter-in-law went to look for the gift shop. I simply stood and meditated in the stillness and quiet.

Three different responses, all good. The miracle at Moraine Lake was my clarity to let people be who they are and do what they do. There's something for everyone, and it's all good.

Exercise 8-29: When have you experienced this level of acceptance?

8-30: Clearing

Last night's sky was so clear that I easily saw the Pleides and Orion's Belt.

I know at this moment, medical personnel are in harm's way. Clerks are stocking grocery shelves. Truckers are barreling down highways and through neighborhoods to deliver what our lives need for sustenance. Financial advisors and business owners are absorbing stress. For all these, I pray for their safety and give thanks for their effort and dedication.

In my world, all is calm. My calendar is blank. No meetings. No must-have's. I'm spending more time outdoors, paying attention to what the plants need, taking the dog for regular walks, eliminating what is not necessary. Even in the midst of danger, I feel peace. That's the power of clearing.

Exercise 8-30: What is your experience with clearing? What needs to be cleared right now, from your mind or physical environment?

8-31: Slowing Down During the Pandemic

I give thanks that my family and friends are well. I pray for those who are not and for those who minister to them. May they sense God's presence and ease into grace.

As for me, when my calendar cleared, I slowed down. I've realized that nothing has to be done right now. My home is imperfectly clean, and that's okay. What stopped for me is consumerism. Now, when I think I need something, I don't order it. I think, "That will wait—or maybe I don't really *need* it." Of course, I don't "make a run to the store." When I catch myself thinking, "What do I want to eat?" I shift to "What do we have to eat?"

As these changes have happened, something within me found a place of greater peace.

Exercise 8-31: How about you? What happened to your state of mind during the pandemic?

8-32: Be Still

Years ago, I went through a 28-day program for every form of addiction. My drugs of choice were work and seeking people's approval. My roommate's addictions were alcohol and drugs. She struggled with the discipline of this recovery program. Wherever she went was chaos.

Near the end of the program, she burst into our dorm room, frustrated. She had not been able to do a successful third step, "Made a decision to turn our will and our lives over to the care of God." The way she put it was this, "They say I can't leave until I find God."

I was sitting on the little balcony off our room, gazing into the woods, listening to the birds, and wondering at the flowing stream. I didn't know what to say to her, so I remained silent. We sat there together in silence.

After a bit, she straightened. "That's it!" Then she turned to me and said, "Isn't there something in the Bible about being still?"

I responded, "Be still, and know that I am God." (Psalm 46:10) That was the aha moment that the directors of the program had been looking for in her.

I share this because our addictions are calling to us—our addictions to a bustling, frantic way of life. Our addiction to being with other people to distract us. Our addiction to work to give us a sense of worth. Our addiction to being able to have what we want when we want it.

Exercise 8-32: What is your experience with "Be still, and know that I am God"?

8-33: Blessing of These Times

On a walk this week, we came upon a woman in a hat and sunglasses, waiting for her dog (Miss Kitty) to relieve herself, so Harlan struck up a conversation.

Before long, we discovered we knew several of the same people from my days in Texas education. Then, as I listened more carefully, I realized I had this same conversation with a woman I met at a neighborhood party a couple of years ago—a gathering of about 75 people, all talking loudly, eating, and drinking.

Having the same conversation with the same person in nature's quiet, was actually a different conversation. I could take in her words and reminisce about those people we knew in common. I felt I knew my fellow walker in a new way.

Parties—crowds—noise—visual stimuli—are distractions that keep me from fully focusing on what someone is saying.

Exercise 8-33: When do you have the best conversations?

8-34: Blank Slate

Yesterday I finished the final task of a project that has consumed me for two years. In the next month and a half, I'll finish another major responsibility.

I'm looking at a blank slate.

Grandma Moses started painting at the age of 78, after her sister-in-law suggested it. She painted 1500 works of art before she died at the age of 101.

I've been told I am "gifted with words," so my new focus is writing. I wonder what I'll create.

Exercise 8-34: When have you had a blank slate? What did you do with it?

Chapter 9 - Light Has Come into the World

Imagine a tropical rain forest. Leaves are every imaginable shade of green, leaves overlapping each other, with wet drops everywhere. Yet, through a small opening in the canopy, light like a golden floodlight finds its way to the ground.

9-1: The Trail of Life

Where I live in Sedona are many hiking trails. They ascend, descend, and fork. They vary in difficulty. They wind around forests, streams, and rocks. They change with the seasons and weather and time of day. Big rocks sometimes move unexpectedly into the paths, as well as branches. Rains shift the terrain. Even experienced hikers sometimes get lost or stranded.

So it is with life. Sometimes even the guides among us—ministers, intuitives, leaders—lose their way and need help.

On this trail of life, my goal is to live in serenity. I've gotten myself in shape for maintaining peace of mind. I've followed a map that includes daily journaling to get troublesome thoughts out of my mind and onto paper so I can be rid of them. Each morning I meditate and set an intention for the day. Throughout my day, I am aware of what I'm thinking and feeling so that I make constant adjustments, keeping myself on the path and not wandering. To end the day, I express gratitude.

Sometimes my life's trail takes a turn I didn't expect, want, or choose. Sometimes a big boulder blocks my way. Sometimes I have to wait. Sometimes I need help. That's when I make a phone call to a trusted advisor, listen carefully to the calmness in her voice, take a deep breath, and resume my journey.

Exercise 9-1: Right now, what is your life's trail like? Describe it. What will you do?

9-2: Pink Muhly

> The fall grasses bloom in feathers.
> Shimmering whites, yellows—spun straw.
> But when I see the gossamer of pink muhly glow,
> My heart sings.

Exercise 9-2: What makes your heart sing?

9-3: Relief from Burden

Many mornings begin with journaling for me, followed by meditation. Always, I begin by writing what I'm grateful for. Usually I write about a page, unburdening myself with thoughts and feelings that get in the way of my peace.

This morning, after I wrote what I'm grateful for, I wrote only one sentence: "Relieve me from the burden of wanting other people to be different."

Exercise 9-3: What one wish would unburden you?

9-4: You Be You, and I'll Be Me

My daughter bought a tee shirt with the words, "You be you, and I'll be me," which truly reflects her outlook on life and her relationships with other people.

Much of our distress is caused from disappointment when other people don't do—or think—or behave the way we want them to.

Much emotional pain is released when we simply ask, "Am I being the person I want to be?" and leave others to answer that question for themselves.

Exercise 9-4: In what ways are you being the person you truly want to be?

9-5: The Power of Intention

The power of intention became real for me on a day when I asked to "be open for all the love that is here for me." Then I spent the day among people I hadn't seen for years and who I thought might not be happy to see me. Instead, love flowed abundantly and freely around, within, and through me for the rest of the day.

I follow the work of Lynne McTaggart, an investigative reporter by training who works with scientists all over the world to measure the power of intention. The results show unmistakable positive impact, just as I experienced on that day.

Exercise 9-5: Have you experienced the power of intention? If so, what happened? If not, what intention would you like to see materialize?

9-6: Getting to Bliss

Have you ever had the sense that, like a magnet, good things were coming to you effortlessly? That's what I mean by "bliss."

Once I had a lengthy, heart-to-heart conversation with a trusted friend. I shared something that has been a burden on my heart for years, and I finally was able to get to such deep feelings that a door opened and a pathway emerged. After the conversation, I was exhausted. I slept well.

The next morning, I experienced bliss. Symptoms of tension I had been experiencing disappeared. When I went to the drug store, there was no line. I was thirty minutes early to a hair appointment, but as I walked up to the shop, there were three friends enjoying coffee in the beautiful morning. So I sat down to enjoy the conversation with them.

Bliss.

Exercise 9-6: Have you ever experienced the freedom and exultation and happy coincidences that come from speaking your deep truth?

9-7: Energy

Following Harlan's medical urgency and subsequent surgery, after the terror had subsided, I felt exhausted and empty. I had neglected doing what feeds my soul.

Lunch with a friend started reviving me, and I became freshly aware of the power of the energy I allow to come and go into my being.

This morning I awoke disgruntled after a restless night. Unwilling to start my day with that energy, I made a list of friends and the strength I see in each of them. Until I can find my own footing again, I will float on the goodness of others.

Exercise 9-7: What do you do to shift your energy?

9-8: Earth Day

> I put my glasses down
> And my phone,
> Realizing there is no good news.
> Then my eyes turn to the

Window, opening a view of
Grasses, water, trees, and sky
That's where the good news is.

Exercise 9-8: What effect does nature have on you? How much access to nature do you have?

9-9: Keep It Fresh

Along the way, someone told me, "Not everyone who has been driving for thirty years is a good driver."

When we're learning something new, it's easy to be open, creative, alert, and responsive. But when we're doing something we've done for years, it's tempting to be rigid.

My intention for my life is to keep it fresh.

Exercise 9-9: What has become a bit stale or slimy for you? What might you do differently to refresh your life?

9-10: Hearing and Seeing

One of my all-time favorite television shows, before it was cancelled, was "God Friended Me." In this show, a Facebook friend called "God" sends friend suggestions to a young man named Miles, who called himself an atheist, and his two friends. They then find the suggested friend, who always needs help that they can give.

Some days I feel like I'm living in that television show. Only God's suggestions don't show up on Facebook; they just present themselves, and then I realize that I'm in exactly the right place at exactly the right time. I can't explain how this happens. I only know that if I keep myself open to the flow of spirit and open my heart to see and hear what is, the flow of Spirit appears.

Exercise 9-10: How does the flow of Spirit appear for you?

9-11: Ask Someone

My granddaughter and I had just left the 9/11 memorial in New York City, and it was lunchtime. I turned to her saying, "I have no idea how to find a restaurant." She was undaunted. "Ask someone, Nana," she said. So I did, and we had one of the best meals of our trip.

Exercise 9-11: Does something have you stymied? Who will you ask for help?

9-12: Small Kindness

When I was young, I remember hearing, "Make a name for yourself." In other words, go accomplish something. Get a title. A following. Find a solution.

Over time, I've learned that this philosophy of life does not bring me peace.

What does bring peace is small acts of kindness among untitled people: an encouraging word, shared prayer, a small donation, offering a hand.

No longer do I look for a savior leader or long to be one. Rather, I take comfort in realizing there are millions of acts of small kindness happening every day. Every hour. Every minute. Right now.

Exercise 9-12: What are some simple acts of kindness you've observed or experienced in the last twenty-four hours?

9-13: One Day at a Time

Twenty years ago, Harlan and I embarked on programs of recovery based upon the twelve steps. One of the first slogans we learned was "one day at a time." Most of the time we truly live in the day, not worrying about what lies ahead or what is outside of our control. It's been so helpful to both of us to be "on the same page" because when one of us slips, the other is there to remind to stay in the moment.

Exercise 9-13: What do you do to stay out of worry?

9-14: Narrowing? Or Expanding?

Sometimes I think of discipline as narrowing—getting back between the lines, so to speak. I associate the word with constricting.

In a recent meditation with friends, this concept completely changed. I had a dream about a house where I was staying. My room was in the front of the house. When I decided to explore, I found room after room after room. This house was huge! Every room was furnished, but not with more than was needed.

In the meditation, which we worded as "We discard toxicity and choose what is good, truthful, and pure," what came to me was this scripture: "In my father's house are many mansions."

Now I think of discipline as expanding.

Exercise 9-14: How do you think of discipline? What is the role of discipline in your life?

Chapter 10 - Silent Striated Sentinel

Imagine a wall of stone, with dark and light striations, standing as if a sentinel, noiselessly observing all that is.

10-1: Step into the Dream

In a few weeks my friend will receive his doctorate from the University of Texas at Austin. This would be a significant accomplishment for anyone, but even more so for my friend, who is dyslexic. Academic achievement hasn't come easily for him, yet for years he has chipped unresentfully away at it, happily and doggedly in pursuit of his dream.

When he graduates, he will wear a robe. As he crosses the stage to receive his diploma, a university official will place a hood around his neck in the color of his academic discipline. From that moment on, his life will be forever changed.

My neighbor told me last night of her fascination in watching lady bugs be born on her vinca plants. First, she sees eggs on the leaves. About a week later, they are larva. Almost a month later comes the pupa stage. Finally, a ladybug crawls out. At first, she is solid red. Later the black spots appear, and she steps into the fullness of her life.

It's inspiring to watch man and nature step into a dream.

Exercise 10-1: What dream are you or someone you love stepping into? What feelings does that evoke in you?

10-2: Waft

Sedona vortex expert Pete Sanders taught me a way to meditate that yields my word for the day. The word that came up was unusual—waft.

It's not a word I use, so I looked it up. It means "carried on the breeze, as a scent." That definition brought to mind a childhood memory of honeysuckle growing on my grandmother's fence, its sweet fragrance wafting through the air, lifting my spirits and awakening my senses.

Exercise 10-2: What lifts your spirits and awakens your senses? What is "wafting" for you?

10-3: One Day at a Time

As I sit on my patio in the cool of the morning, gazing with my heart at the magnificence of Bell Rock and Courthouse Butte, I wonder, "Oh, God, how did I get here?"

This morning a quiet voice answered, "One day at a time."

I realize everything I treasure has come to me one day at a time: peace of mind, a happy marriage, treasured friendships and family relationships, health and well-being.

The thrill of those "big" goals I grasped for—career, projects, purchases—is gone.

What remains is silent majesty. Quiet presence. One day at a time.

Exercise 10-3: What treasures have come to you one day at a time?

10-4: Faith

This morning the clouds are so low that I can't see the familiar red rocks or the red rays of sunrise. Yet I know they are there, beyond what I can see.

Exercise 10-4: What do you know is there, beyond what you can see?

10-5: Decision

On the very day that Harlan celebrated his sixteenth year of sobriety in AA, we took communion at church. If the liquid in the tiny little cup is red, it's wine. If it's clear, it's grape juice. Harlan and I always choose the clear liquid.

On this Sunday, I saw when the server came to me, that there was only one cup of grape juice left, and Harlan had yet to be served. I hesitated. Then I said to myself, "Well, I haven't had alcohol in sixteen years, either. Let him figure it out for himself."

He did. He leaned forward and said to the server, "I need grape juice." Quickly, he was served.

What I've learned in this journey of recovery with him is that, when I take care of myself, things work out well for everyone. I've learned that this is not selfishness but self-care, a contagious act of self-respect. I've also learned that sometimes when we "overhelp" others, we send a message that we don't believe they can do it for themselves.

Exercise: Is there anyone you are "overhelping"? What are you doing to take care of yourself?

10-6: Signs of Daybreak

The blue-gray hills
Shadow the sun's rise.
In the soft clouds above,

I see growing signs of daybreak.

Exercise10-6: What signs of change are happening around you?

10-7: Surfing My Calendar

I just forwarded through my calendar to the end of the year, noting the recurring events and the special ones, as well. Travel. Visits. Appointments.

What doesn't appear on my calendar are the most important aspects of my life—the love I have for Harlan as he heads for the golf course, the compassion I feel for a young woman who trustingly expresses her anguish to me.

May God surf me through these days, whatever events they bring, with love and compassion.

Exercise 10-7: Thumb forward through your calendar. What energy is surfing you through it?

10-8: I Choose Peace

I read the headlines in the digital version of the Washington Post hurriedly, feeling the stress of ominous words and fear-filled events or dreads. Then I look up, out my bedroom window to the gentle hills, peaceful pond, and soft, early morning light. Once again, I realize my state of mind is my choice. Once again, I choose peace.

Exercise 10-8: Have you noticed the effect the day's news has on you? What do you do to keep your state of mind peaceful?

10-9: Perfectly Timed Encouragement

I awoke to find a posting on Facebook from someone who was in my sophomore English class oh, so many years ago. How did she know that her kind, affirming words were exactly what I needed to hear today?

Next week I will teach the first in a four-class series in personal growth. It's been awhile since I've done anything like this, and I've been wondering if I'll be effective, or if anyone will even sign up. After all, I've lived in Sedona only seven months, and few people know me.

Then I learned that the class did have enough students sign up, and the very next morning I awoke to a strong affirmation from a gracious student from my past.

Courage awakened in me as I realized how much I love teaching. My former student's encouragement came at exactly the right time, and I'm grateful.

Exercise 10-9: Tell the story of when encouragement came for you at exactly the right time.

10-10: Simplicity and Peace

I spent much of my life making things happen—doing projects—charting my course.

Today I focus on my breathing—live in gratitude—and wait for the path to appear.

Simplicity and peace.

Exercise 10-10: How do you spend your life? Is there anything you'd like to change?

10-11: The Energy of Things

I look around my bedroom as I awaken to my photograph of light coming through a Hawaiian rainforest. As my eyes pan the room, there's an exquisite Asian beaded wall hanging, a gift from a grateful friend. Two small angels, gifts from friends, look down from a high shelf. Simply looking at these treasures evokes, love, pleasure, and adventure. As I awaken, my spirit lifts.

I hear a lot these days about our relationship with things. I choose to be selectively surrounded with what brings out the best in me.

Exercise 10-11: What surrounds you? What does it evoke in you?

10-12: Reconstruction

On this beautiful spring day, two dear people with broken bones begin their recovery from the crash.

The road that leads to our home lies bare, awaiting a new surface.

Reconstruction.

Exercise 10-12: What in your life is being reconstructed? What is the new creation you want to see?

10-13: One Day at a Time

Our friend Tony had cancer from the first time we met him. He was a remarkable man, an expert in agriculture, a bull rider in his youth, and a faithful member of a 12-step recovery group. His favorite slogan, which I heard him say every time I was with him, was "One day at a time."

When his cancer spread and radiation was required, he said, "It's one day at a time." When hip surgery was needed so that he could tour Europe with his wife and grandchildren, he said, "One day at a time." When chemo was administered and another surgery was required, he said, "It's one day at a time." And when he had to be pushed in a wheelchair....

Five months before he died, Tony and his wife Andra hosted a "gratitude party," to express their appreciation for the love and support of friends and family.

The last time Harlan and I spoke with him, two days before he died, he said, "I've come to the end of the road."

In his voice was no trace of resentment; it was simple acceptance.

Never resentment. No anger. His soul was clear. He had lived life on life's terms, one day at a time.

Exercise 10-13: Have you known anyone like our friend Tony? What did they teach you?

10-14: The Path

I took a hike on my favorite trail—only this time I did the hike backward. I started where I usually finish.

The trail looked different. My feet didn't automatically take the steps they had memorized. I had to open my eyes and look closely. The trail curves and arcs, rises and falls. I could see only short distances.

Just like life. We really can't see the whole pathway, only what's in front of us. But many fears and apprehensions are born from trying to see the whole trail.

Today, may you be blessed by focusing only on what's in front of you, one day at a time. Some days, one hour at a time. Some hours, one minute at a time.

Exercise 10-14: What trail are you hiking? What's right in front of you?

10-15: Gift of Presence

One Christmas my father bought a jigsaw puzzle and sat with me for what seemed like hours, carefully eyeing, fingering, and placing the pieces. I learned how exquisite patience and stillness can be. I don't remember what Santa brought that year, but I will never forget the gift of my father's presence.

Exercise 10-15: What is a precious holiday memory from your childhood? What is an instance of being in the presence of a parent's full attention?

10-16: Another Type of Miracle

I was present when the gift of a new computer was presented to a young woman who has had a tough, challenging life, including drug-addicted parents, abandonment, abuse, and her own addictions. Now in her early twenties, sober and the single mother of an infant daughter, she has decided to go back to school and make something good of her life.

Touched by the kindness of the gift, this young woman dissolved into tears, put her head down on the table and sobbed, not regaining composure for several minutes. I sensed that she had not ever received a gift of this magnitude.

As I drove home, I felt I had witnessed a miracle. This morning I read this passage from *A Course in Miracles*: "A major contribution of miracles is their strength in releasing a person from his misplaced sense of isolation, deprivation, and lack." Yes, that's what I saw.

Exercise 10-16: When have you witnessed a miracle? What happened?

10-17: Gemstones

> Royal blue was the color of her youth—
> Sapphire strong, vibrant, fearless.
> Successes came and went, like
> Waves lapping the vast shoreline.
> But for her maturity, aquamarine and pearls
> Chose her, cascading their serenity,
> Peace, and calm
> Among the sands and rocks of the cove.

Exercise 10-17: What gemstones represent you, then and now?

10-18: Nature Speaks

> Morning sun shining
> Through pink feathery grass
> Tells my soul that all is well

Exercise 10-18: How does nature speak to you? What does she say?

10-19: Dawdling

Dawdling is getting things done without a to-do list. It's floating from task to task, effortlessly. Dawdling is living without have-to's. It's trusting myself to do what is right in the moment.

Exercise 10-19: Do you ever dawdle? How does it seem to you?

10-20: The Listener

When I was a little girl, after supper (that's what we called it), I would go to the swing on Mrs. McCall's front porch. She was always there, our next-door neighbor, silently swinging back and forth. I would sit beside her, downloading everything that happened to me that day—at school, with friends. I could say anything to her without fear of reprimand or belittling. I must have chattered away, filling all the time and space, because I do not remember one word Mrs. McCall ever said to me. Yet, I will never forget her for letting me do all the talking. When I was a child, I needed that. Sometimes, I still do.

Exercise 10-20: Who was a listener for you? For whom are you a listener?

10-21: Unfolding

Maybe it's the time of year—a time when I see graduation postings on Facebook in abundance—postings of beautiful young women I remember as toddlers or adolescents. Seeing them in cap and gown seems a sharp change, a clear break from what used to be into what is yet to be.

It's startling only because I missed the gradual, gentle unfolding of one phase of these lives into the next.

Exercise 10-21: What is unfolding for you? What is startling for you?

10-22: Feeling the Feelings

For a long time in my life, I shut down my emotions. Of course, I suffered the consequences, most notably migraine headaches. Someone who was helping me recover my whole self, asked me, in response to a statement I had made, "How do you feel about this?" I answered her. She said, "You just told me what you think. I asked how you feel." I couldn't answer her question.

Once when a family member died, I grabbed a broom and swept the driveway, to avoid feeling. This was a favorite strategy—stay busy; don't feel.

Last week, anticipating my Harlan's triple bypass surgery, I was scared. I cried. Several times. As they pushed him into surgery, I broke down. For a while I was very tired from the range of emotions coursing through me—gratitude for the skill of his medical team and for the progress he is making, anger and sadness that we have to go through this, appreciation for the friends who have come to our aid, apprehension about what our lives will be like going forward—and rejoicing that I am able to feel my feelings.

Wise people have taught me that feelings pass. I don't have to act on them. But for my own health, I do need to feel them.

Exercise 10-22: What do you do with your feelings?

10-23: Stay Unlocked

For the first time in my life, I have bedroom windows with an eastern view, so I watch the sunrise every morning. Earth's rotation assures that the sun never rises in exactly the same place from day to day, and I have to close different blinds through the year to accommodate the rotation of the rising sun's rays.

There's a saying that "we never step in the same river twice, for the water is constantly flowing."

Motion—change—is the natural order.

Exercise 10-23: What's moving in your life? Does any part of your life feel "locked"? What would you like to do about it?

10-24: The Power of Respectful Listening

It was a simple invitation to dessert in the evening in my friend's home. I prepared for light, trivial conversation. But one of the guests was interested in the work I had done in my career. I tried to answer casually, as one does in social settings, but he probed, maintained eye contact, and listened carefully as I told the fuller story.

I left my friend's home that evening bathed in grace and blessed by someone who truly listened and respected what I had to say.

Exercise 10-24: When have you been listened to with respect? When have you been a respectful listener?

10-25: How the Light Gets In

I had placed my trust in something that failed. I was devastated and heartbroken, so I asked for help.

Help came through art created by Ash Almonte—through one of Father Richard Rohr's daily meditations that mentioned the Japanese art form that repairs cracks in ceramics with gold. I followed every lead, opening my heart for truth and love in every message. The process led me to this scripture: "Where sin increased, grace abounded all the more" (Romans 5:20).

It also led me to these words by Leonard Cohen: "Ring the bells that still can ring. Forget your perfect offering. There is a crack in everything. That's how the light gets in."

Exercise 10-25: What do you do when you're heartbroken?

10-26: Another Pass at Letting Go

I've been reading from the *Tao Te Ching* by Stephen Mitchell keep coming back to these lines: "If you want to shrink something, you must first allow it to expand. If you want to get rid of something, you must first allow it to flourish."

In Al-Anon, I've learned the slogan, "Let go and let God."

In the Bible, I read, "Be still and know that I am God."

But reading this new language to express the same powerful truth has deepened it within me.

May you let go of expectations and experience perfect peace. All truly is well.

Exercise 10-26: What experience have you had with letting go? What happened?

10-27: Floating

I love working jigsaw puzzles. Wooden ones. The pieces of a wooden puzzle are interesting and fit together in unusual ways.

When I try to "figure out" what goes where in a wooden puzzle, it doesn't work. But when I just sit back and look for awhile, content not to know, eventually my hands start moving, and some pieces fit together. It's as if another part of my brain works on its own, without help from me.

It is a delightful state to be in because it's effortless. In these days, may you be content to simply float in life.

Exercise 10-27: What is floating like for you?

10-28: Pruning

Yesterday I pruned the rose bushes. This morning, as I look out the window, I see streams of light flowing through them and realize, "Now they can breathe!" They seem happier, leaves less crowded.

In these pandemic times, so many are cleaning, clearing, pruning, and setting themselves free from overcrowded schedules, clutter, and obligations. Is it possible that we might be preparing for healthier, happier lives?

At the same time, I'm told that these times are very difficult for people with addictions, and deaths are increasing. This morning my friends and I set this intention: "Prune the addictions that keep us trapped. Set all souls free."

Exercise 10-28: When you hear the word "pruning," what do you visualize? What meaning does the word have for you?

10-29: In Flow

> Dawn breaks.
> Chill autumn morning begins.
> Yet in my heart I know
> These stops and starts are truly continuum.
> The stops and starts are within me.
> I choose to stay in flow.

Exercise 10-29: How is your life continuum? When does it feel like stops and starts? How do you want it to be?

10-30: Being Fully Present

In 2020 I was struck by the presence of Tiger Woods in the Masters award presentation to a new champion. He was fully attentive to everyone's comments. He accepted praise from the amateur champion with silent grace. He seemed genuinely pleased to award the green jacket to his successor.

So often, when I am with others, my mind is wandering. I'm thinking of something else or what I will say next or I'm glancing at my phone.

Tiger Words showed me what being fully present—simply being in the moment—looks like. I like it. I'm setting it as a goal.

Exercise 10-30: Start noticing how present you are with other people—especially people in your family. How do you seem to others? Is it how you want to be?

Appendix

Heart Meditation

Sit in a quiet, private place. Close your eyes. Take three long, deep breaths. Breathe all the way to your navel.

Now place your hand over your heart. Feel the warmth of you hand on your skin, penetrating all the way to your heart. Tune in to the beating of your heart.

Realize that this heart started beating in the third week after your conception. Since that moment, it has been pumping oxygen and nutrients throughout your whole body, sustaining your life.

Thank your heart for so faithfully sustaining your life. Ask your heart to guide you going forward.

Take another deep breath. And another. And another.

When you are ready, open your eyes.

Author's Note

About halfway through compiling the entries for this book, I became uneasy and discouraged. I knew I couldn't continue to write in that state of mind, so I stopped to go outside, do some yard work, and get clear about what was going on with me.

Upon reflection, I realized that when I was growing up, sharing experiences meant talking about what was bad—what someone did wrong—sharing negative judgments about ourselves and others. Someone who shared positive, uplifting experiences, as I have in this book, would have been labeled "uppity" or "big headed" or "self-righteous."

I had to stop writing because I was deafened by the old voice of self-condemnation and limitation.

A bit later, a friend pointed out one of Sedona's red rocks with black areas of "desert varnish," a patina that forms through the years and increases beauty. Then I realized that I could think of these old voices as my "desert varnish." They are part of a pattern that I can notice, appreciate, and walk away from.

The truth is, my state of mind and yours are a choice. And the whole truth is, we attract what we emit. We truly can live the lives we want. My hope is that this book lights the way.

About the Author

Author of *Journey from Head to Heart* and *Alphabet Meditations for Teachers*, Dr. Nancy Oelklaus has spoken throughout the U.S. as well as in Indonesia, Singapore, and The Netherlands. Her articles have appeared in *The Systems Thinker*, *Leverage*, *The American School Board Journal*, *The Austin Business Journal*, and *Leaders of Learners*. Her leadership profile, "The Power of Love," appears in *Appreciative Leaders: In the Eye of the Beholder*, published by the Taos Institute. Her poetry has appeared in numerous publications, including the newsletter of the Story Circle Network and the monograph of the Texas Council of Women School Executives, entitled *Women as School Executives: The Complete Picture* (2000).

Dr. Oelklaus has received numerous awards and honors for civic leadership, including the Vision to Action Award from the Visions of a Better World Foundation in Boston. She was named Leader of Leaders by Sam Houston State University's Department of Educational Leadership, Outstanding Graduate by Texas A&M, Commerce, Department of Educational Leadership, and Woman of Achievement by the Business and Professional Women of Marshall, Texas.

She holds a Doctor of Education degree in educational leadership from Texas A&M University, Commerce, a Master of Arts in English from the University of North

Texas, and a Bachelor of Arts in speech communication, cum laude, from Oklahoma Baptist University.

~ ~ ~

After her college graduation, Dr. Oelklaus married and threw her anchor into the safe harbor of Marshall, Texas, where her husband's family had lived for generations. She pursued advanced education and a career in public education, which, along with motherhood, were very fulfilling.

Then the day came when the children were gone, and she had reached her professional goals in that place. A voice deep within said, "If you don't get out of here, you'll die." In response, she left her career and her marriage.

The next six years were full of change—new city, lots of travel, new career, new homes, new friends, new marriage.

In that second marriage, Nancy decided to stop running from emotional pain and simply go through it. With a lot of help—professional, personal, and Al-Anon—she finally learned that peace comes from within, after truth and taking responsibility.

The meditations in this book come from the simple serenity she lives today in Sedona, AZ.

About the Cover

Artist Ash Almonte and I have been on a spiritual path together for quite a few years, so I asked her to create the cover design for Simple Serenity, even though it's not in her normal line of work. She graciously agreed. On the day she sent her mockup, with soft colors erupting from a red-hot base, I finished Cynthia Bourgeault's wisdom school based on her book, *The Eye of the Heart*. The school, which was a retreat for live participants, utilized thick fishing ropes for those attending to unravel and then intertwine in a large display. The completed display, which I saw for the first time after I received Ash's mockup, was a mass of color—green, yellow, blue, red.

On that same day, my heart friend Jennifer sent me a photograph, taken by her hairdresser, of light streaming through the stained glass windows of La Sagrada Familia Cathedral in Barcelona—again, a mass of vibrant color.

This is how I know that Ash had rightly discerned the image needed for this book. This experience is typical of how I know I am on the right path.

You know those grids on the sides of the highway that tell us we need to make a course correction? Well, our hearts have those grids, too. We call them feelings. When something doesn't feel right, it isn't. It's a sign we need to make an adjustment. On the other hand, when we feel serene, when everything "lines up," life is good and all is well.

The peaceful blue-white experiences of our lives grow out of the cauldron of life.

About the Artist

Cascading color and brave brush strokes are the foundations of the stunning artwork of Ash Almonte. Her bold and risk taking abstract figures and chandeliers are gaining traction in the art world, as they exude feelings of light and joy. Truly, she is incredible.

Ash began her interest in art at a very young age. Growing up with her father working at a fruit stand, she was heavily influenced by vibrant colors and textures. She used found objects often to create small masterpieces, increasing her desire to create. She went on to obtain a Bachelor of Fine Arts from McMurry University in Abilene and here career soared shortly after that. Furthermore, she's uses all sorts of mediums such as acrylics, gels, charcoals, and even enamel. As is visible to her audience, Ash Almonte is fueled by the process of creating, rather than the final result of the piece. The dramatic brush strokes, the thick layers of paint, and cut up pieces of textiles join perfectly together to create her abstract expression paintings.

Ash explains how the theory of light has been an ever-prevalent source of her inspiration. Her work is recognizable for its elaborate and expressive chandeliers. Big and bold, these chandeliers seemingly glow within themselves, and are often coupled with flowers or other attributes that make them even more compelling. She also paints figures, sometimes single and sometimes couples, that are colorful and bright. Bold and brilliant mark-makings make her paintings distinct. Her work could even be described as fashionable impressionism, with its classic technique combined with colors and styles from the fashion industry.

Ash is represented in several galleries in the southwest, as well as various private and public collections around the United States.

> "It is more about the execution, than the final product. I enjoy the process of making art more than the product. I am inspired by beautiful color, incredible music, outrageous fashion, raw works of art, loud works of art, and even by taking risks," says Ash. "I am also moved by the process of change, learning of individuals who are doing good things in the world or for our planet, or even hearing about miraculous stories of the past and present. I am moved by life and inspired by every minute of it."
>
> - Ash Almonte

Bibliography

Alcoholics Anonymous. (2020). *Alcoholics Anonymous big book*. Hawthorne, CA: BN Publishing

Anthony, M. (2021). *The afterlife frequency: The scientific proof of spiritual contact and how that awareness will change your life*. Novato, CA: New World Library

Bourgeault, C. (2003). *The wisdom way of knowing: Reclaiming an ancient tradition to awaken the heart*. San Francisco, CA: Jossey-Bass.

Bourgeault, C. (2020). *Eye of the heart: A spiritual journey into the imaginal realm*. Boulder, CO: Shambhala Publications.

Dalai Lama & Desmond Tutu. (2016). *The Book of Joy:* New York: Random House.

Foster, R. J. (2005). *The Renovaré Spiritual formation Bible: New Revised Standard version with Deutero-canonical books*. San Francisco: HarperSanFrancisco.

Frankl, V. E. (1980). *Man's search for meaning*. Redwood City, Calif: Woodside Terrace Kiwanis Club.

Hawkins, D. R. (2002). *Power vs. force: The hidden determinants of human behavior*. Carlsbad, Calif: Hay House.

Leloup, J., & Leloup, J. (2002). *Gospel of mary magdalene*. Rochester, VT: Inner Traditions International.

Mackesy, C. (2021). *The boy, the mole, the fox and the horse*. New York: HarperOne.

McTaggart, L. (2008). *The field: The quest for the secret force of the universe*. New York: Harper.

McTaggart, L. (2019). *The power of eight: Harnessing the miraculous energies of a small group to heal others, your life and the world*. Carlsbad, CA: Hay House.

Mitchell, S. (2019). *Joseph and the way of forgiveness: A biblical tale retold*. New York: St. Martin's Essentials.

Mitchell, S. (1988). *Tao Te Ching By Stephen Mitchell*. New York: Harper Collins.

Rohr, R. (2019). *The universal Christ: How a forgotten reality can change everything we see, hope for, and believe*. New York: Random House.

Rohr, R., In Chase, J., & In Traeger, J. (2018). *Richard Rohr: Essential teachings on love*. Maryknoll, NY:Orbis Books.

Rose, S. (2003). *She let go - poem by Safire Rose*. Safire Rose. Retrieved February 21, 2022, from https://safire-rose.com/books-and-media/poetry/she-let-go

Sanders, P. A. (1992). *Scientific vortex information: How to easily understand, find, and tap vortex energy in Sedona and wherever you travel!*. Sedona, Ariz: Free Soul.

Thoreau, H. D., (2012). *Walden, or Life in the woods: And On the duty of civil disobedience*. Seattle: Loki Publishing.

Index

acceptance, 36, 41, 63
Adams, A., 94
ADHD, 23
alcoholism, 23
Almonte, A., 37, 111, 136
attitude, 60
authenticity, 58
being present, 61, *131*
being true to myself, 57
Blatner, D., 34
blessing, 50
bliss, 119
carefree, 50
ceiling fan, 11
chaos, 6, 33
character defects, 59
choice, 104
Christmas, 20, 21, 103, 108, 131
clarity, 70
Cohen, L., 136
companion, 86
controversy, 58
Curry, J., 34
dawdling, 45, 108
de Chardin, T., 73
Desiderata, 62
disappointment, 9, 76
divinity, 41
dream, 49
Dutch babies, 98
Eastwood, C., 35
Ehrmann, M., 62

emergence, 71
energy, 120
equanimity, 7
everyone wins, 65
expectation, 52
facing challenge, 72
faith, 35, 60, *127*
feel your feelings, 74
flow, 104
focus, 78
forgiveness, 72, 74, 75, 82
Frankl, V., 35
friendship, 85
funk, 34
generosity, 20
gifts, 26
gliding, 20
good day, 45
grace, 38, 91
gratitude, 11, 17
harmony, 29
Hawkins, D., 63, 64
hawks, 25
help, 83
help, accepting, 31
holy place, 78
hostage, 14
hula hoop, 52
humility, 34
impatience, 90
incremental shifts, 43
intention, 119
jigsaw puzzle, 30

judgmentalism, 27
Keith, T., 35
kindness, 38, 122
leaving, 8, 13
Leloup, J.Y., 68
Let it be, 56
let life be life, 40
lists, 13
love, 66
lull, 102
Mackesy, C., 83
manzanita bush, 48
McTaggert, L., 66
measuring worth, 31
meditation, 103, 106
Medoff, M., 110
memorable person, 67
minding own business, 24
mirror, 29
mistakes, 36
Mitchell, S., *136*
Mogollon Rim, 78
mushiness, 23
Mustin, J.F., iii
native language, 62
negative thinking, 66
Nemeth, M., 82
Olsen, B.L., 3
opportunity, 39
overwhelm, 10
peer pressure, 40
perfect day, 46
perfectionism, 47
pink muhly, 118
play, 49
powerlessness, 111
Prator, J.G., 35

priorities, 49
props, 19
pruning, *137*
reconstruction, *130*
Red Rock Pathway, 2, 61
Restorative Justice, 81
rewrite the script, 44
rewriting the script, 47
rhythm, 12
Rinpoche, J.I., 19
Rohr, R., 136
Ruiz, M., 64
Saint Louis Basilica, 51
Sanders, P., 2, 126
savoring, 47
Segall, L., 79
Shakespeare, 29
snow, 87
sobriety, *127*
Socrates, 58
standards, 56
stillness, 114
Tagore, R., 9
Tao Te Ching, *136*
Thanksgiving, 87
Thoreau, D., 110
threading the needle, 80
transformation, 55
trespasses, 35
Tulsa Massacre, 68
turbulence, 28
unfolding, *134*
unlearning, 97
wardrobe, 15
wholeness, 36
wordless sharing, 61
workaholism, 90

Journey From Head to Heart is...

Journey from Head to Heart

HEAD WAY

HEART WAY

Living and Working Authentically

NANCY OELKLAUS

- A Toolkit for those who are exhausted from solving never-ending problems, working harder and harder and not arriving at the destination where they truly want to be.

- A Map for how to make the journey from head to heart and then integrate the two so that the power of ego is diminished and the Authentic Self can emerge to live and work from the power of the human spirit.

- A Reference book you can use for many years to come as the reader meets life's challenges with success that satisfies both the head and the heart.

Journey from Head to Heart is exactly that, integrating logic, reason, emotion, spirituality, recovery, science, and ancient wisdom from a variety of sources to create a recipe for wholeness. The tools and processes are designed for people who are a little wary of "touchy-feely" or "New Age" approaches.

"For beginners on a spiritual voyage, as well as for experienced travelers, Journey From Head To Heart is very powerful. I couldn't put it down. Its stories, told with clarity and simplicity, make it a treasure."
—Dr. Linda O'Neal, Executive Director, Southwest Education Alliance

From Loving Healing Press

Alphabet Meditations: Everyday Wisdom for Educators

Readers of these meditations will get back in touch with why they wanted to teach in the first place—because they care about kids and want to make a meaningful contribution to their lives. By using these meditations with the guide at the end of the book, teachers will:

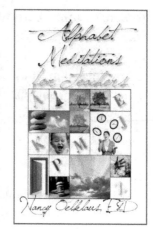

- Sharpen intuitive abilities.

- Through letting go, watch issues be resolved easily.

- Simply enjoy relationships with students, parents, and colleagues.

- Enjoy teaching more by focusing on what's really important.

- Be peaceful, regardless of what is going on.

"*Alphabet Meditations for Teachers* is a most needed antidote to the toxic side effects of our accumulated reactions to institutional rigidity and regimentation; to models of efficiency that privilege technocratic instruction over meaningful and organic teaching and learning."
--Caroline Eick, Ph.D., Assistant Professor, Education Department, Mount St. Mary's University, Emmitsburg, MD

From Loving Healing Press